Globalization and Social Change

Published by :
Lotus Press Publishers & Distributors

Globalization and Social Change

Sanjeev Mahajan

Lotus Press

4735/22, Prakash Deep Building
Ansari Road, Darya Ganj,
New Delhi - 110002

Lotus Press : Publishers & Distributors
Unit No. 220, 2nd Floor, 4735/22, Prakash Deep Building,
Ansari Road, Darya Ganj, New Delhi- 110002
Ph.: 23280047, 98118-38000
• E-mail : lotuspress1984@gmail.com
www.lotuspress.co.in

Globalization and Social Change

ISBN: 81-8382-067-0

Printed & Published by : **Lotus Press Publishers & Distributors,** New Delhi-2

Contents

Introduction

Globalization has ushered plethora of studies. This process refers to mutual interdependence of the countries of the world, particularly their economic interdependence and freedom to integrate with one another through trade, investments and capital flows. Globalization has economic, political, social, cultural and several other dimensions and has made tremendous impact across cultures. In fact, this process has changed the world scenario and cultural landscape of our planet. This has rendered the world into a 'global village'.

The present book dwells upon this important process taking place in almost all the countries of the world. Contributors to this theme have shown new insights about globalization. Alvin Y. So, in the first article has analyzed the communist path of developmental state in the light of Chinese experience. She has argued that the prospect for the China's development depends very much on how the Chinese developmental state handles the problems of socialist transition and the problems of reintegration into the world economy.

Ayodele Samuel Jegede and others have tried to explore the impact of the HIV/AIDS epidemic on the entire population in Africa and highlight its consequences for development in the second article. They have emphasized the need for international cooperation in prevention and control of HIV/AIDS.

The third article of Janja Zitnik deals with globalization and the prospects of multi-cultural coexistence and world peace in the light of Slovenia. It has been shown that a global multi-cultural coexistence and peace can never be achieved unless they are based on a just socio-economic world order.

Stef Aupers and Dick Houtman have dwelled upon oriental religion in the secular West in the light of globalization, new age and the re-enchantment of the world in the fourth article. They have concluded that the Christian churches have declined considerably, whereas new age as a post-traditional type of religion has remarkably increased during the same period in the West.

The fifth article by Joseph M. Conforti on 'The Sweatshop as an Element of National Development: China as a Case in Point' deals with the emergence of sweatshops, the Chinese road to capitalism, factors underlying the development of sweatshops in China and its implications. It has been shown that the conditions under which people are working in the sweatshop factories of south-eastern China are clearly horrible at the individual level, yet they serve the larger society well in relation to an accelerated demographic and industrial transition.

The sixth article of Sanman Jain and others on 'Threshold Effects of Globalization on Poverty, Unemployment, Youth and Religion in India' is the attempt to touch the effects of major domestic issues because of the entry of globalization. The most important issues like poverty and unemployment, lack of technical and skilled training, the impact of global media on youth, family values and radical changes, social upheavals: crime and violence, sex and moral decay, young women's issues: prostitution, aids, abortion, abuse and migration from rural to urban and from India to other countries are dealt with.

Susheel Kumar and Manju Lata in the seventh article on 'Globalization, Multinationals and the Indian Private Sector' have shown that if Indian companies invest more in product quality and customer services, they would certainly succeed in taking any challenge, big or small, in the wake of globalization.

Hemlata Sharma and her colleagues have analyzed social change by education among Scheduled Castes in the era of globalization in India in the eighth article. They have shown that education acts as a cause and determinant of social change, education can also be cause of social change and can be effected by social change, but urbanization does influence the nature of social change.

Surabhi Mahajan in ninth article on 'Impact of Globalization and Liberalization on Zari Embroidery in India' traces the origin of globalization and liberalization in India and tries to find out the impact of these processes on zari embroidery. She has concluded that though zari industry has withstood the challenge of globalization and liberalization, yet the socio-economic conditions of zari workers have remained unchanged.

Malti Phogat has analyzed the impact of globalization on agrarian social structure in Western Uttar Pradesh, a prosperous region of northern India, in tenth article. She has shown how the traditional relationships between landowners, farmers and landless people have changed in this region.

Rajul Datt and his colleagues have analyzed the impact of globalization on transfer of knowledge in cultural perspective in eleventh article. They have shown that the global companies buy from the cheapest markets and sell where they can get maximum prices, i.e. globalization calls for reduction of costs, improvement of quality, expansion of markets and diversification into new areas and markets. To take advantage of global markets, Indian companies are making strategic alliances with foreign companies.

The twelfth article of Priyanka Kapoor on 'Globalization : Conceptual Framework and Transition' has clarified different connotations of globalization, its major players, nature and existence of globalization, its characteristics, globalization, pro-globalization (globalism) and the transition to global society.

A. B. Lal has analyzed emerging trends of the impact of globalization on cross-border capital flows in the thirteenth article. He has shown that globalization has both positive and negative aspects. The country with efficient economic management will face less of negative aspects and more of the positive aspects.

Sanjeev Mahajan in the last article on 'Globalization and Social Change' has tried to show that globalization is a new process capable of explaining social change better than its earlier conceptions like evolution, development, progress, westernization and modernization. He has also pointed out the positive and negative consequences of this process for Indian society.

1

The Communist Path of Developmental State : The Chinese Experience

Alvin Y. So*

1. Introduction

In the literature on East Asian development, the East Asian developmental states in South Korea and Taiwan are seen as the good guys, while the Chinese communist state is seen as the bad guy. The argument is that although the above states were backward and poor in the 1950s, South Korea and Taiwan have developed in a very rapid rate. By the 1980s, South Korea and Taiwan became Newly Industrializing Economies (NIEs) and their states become developmental states. By the 1990s, South Korea and Taiwan further upgraded to East Asian developmental miracles, and they have become the developmental model for countries in the South to emulate.

On the other hand, China remained backward and poor during the period that her East Asian neighbours had taken off. The Chinese communist project is evaluated to be a disaster. China's Great Leap Forward in the late 1950s is reported to have led to famine and the death of millions of people. Her Cultural Revolution (1966-1975) is said to have turned the Chinese society upside down, resulting in political anarchy. Besides, China is said to have experienced the structural problems of a planned

* Division of Social Science, Hong Kong University of Science and Technology, Clear Water Bay, Kowloon, Hong Kong.

economy. China's state enterprises are labeled as highly inefficient because they paid little heed to productivity, had been operating under a "soft budgetary constraint", and could rely on the state for more subsidies if they ran into losses. Subsequently, China's state enterprises are criticized for stocking up more resources and manpower than necessary, leading to waste, misuse of resources, and acute shortages of raw materials.

This paper will re-examine this familiar story of successful East Asian developmental states versus the failed Chinese communist state. It argues that both states are actually the historical products of the Cold War and U.S. hegemonic struggles in the East Asia. It further argues that although the Chinese communist state failed to promote economic growth, the revolutionary Maoist project had constructed a strong party-state, promoted an intensive nationalist ideology, built up local infrastructure and institutions, and incurred no foreign debt, thus laying the foundation for its metamorphosis into a developmental state in the post-1978 reform era. However, having a communist origin, the Chinese developmental state has faced a different set of developmental problems from those facing the East Asian development states. At the end, this paper contends that the rospect for the Chinese developmental state depends on how it resolves the problems of socialist transitions and the problems of reintegration into the capitalist world-economy.

To begin our discussion, it may be helpful to provide a critical review of the concept of East Asian developmental states.

2. Deconstructing the East Asian Developmental States

As a critique of the neoclassical economic perspective, the statist literature[1] argues that it is the developmental state—not the market—that explains the success of East Asian development. Developmental states are distinguished by the fact that their bureaucratic elites have actively intervened in the economy, such as targeting industries for subsidizes, protecting domestic markets from foreign imports, and promoting exports to the global markets. The statist literature tends to stress the technical competence of bureaucratic elites; they are able to formulate strategic developmental policies because they are recruited "from among the technically most highly qualified people in the system." In addition, bureaucratic elites are shielded from the political pressures of various interest groups, making the developmental state highly autonomous.

In highlighting the technical nature and the economic success of East Asian developmental states, the statist literature may have unintentionally overlooked their power configuration, their authoritarianism, and their geopolitical origins[2]. Therefore, instead of taking East Asian developmental states for granted, this paper will critically evaluate their definition, explore why some states want to put economic growth as their top priority, inquire what makes East Asian developmental states strong and autonomous, and look into the dark side of the developmental states.

In the following discussion, it will argue that the Cold War and U.S. hegemonic struggles with communism had played a very important role in the genesis of the developmental states in South Korea and Taiwan. We must bring the Cold War dynamics back in so as to understand the origins, the distinguished features, and the trajectory of East Asian developmental states.

What is a Developmental State and When does it Happen? By definition, a developmental state is one in which its bureaucratic elites put economic growth as its highest priority. In a developmental state, bureaucratic elites will consume all their energy in promoting economic growth, despite this goal will be attained only at the expense of other important goals, such as equality, welfare, democracy, and human rights.

Moreover, although many states aspire to be developmental, only a few will succeed at the end. In this respect, we will not know whether a state is developmental until after the fact, i.e., after the state has gained rapid economic growth and being labeled as a Newly Industrializing Economy (NIE) several decades later. For example, in the 1950s and 1960s there was always a doubt whether the South Korean industrialization was real or it will break down in the near future. It was only in the 1980s after South Korea had become a NIE that researchers agreed to label South Korea as having a developmental state.

Why a State Wants to be Developmental? Every state, of course, wants to promote economic growth. But why did some states want to promote economic growth so desperately that they are willing to sacrifice other important goals in order to attain this one? On this issue, Woo-Cumings[3] insightfully points out that East Asian developmental states are a historical product of war and revolutionary nationalism. It was World War II and the Cold War that brought the issues of nationalism and national survival to the forefront, as Japan was defeated by the U.S., and Korea and China were turned into divided nations. The developmental states were then conceived as a revolutionary project to make these nations strong and powerful, so they could survivel (in the case of South Korea and Taiwan) or catch up with the West (as in the case of Japan).

This emergency situation during the Cold War helps to understand why East Asian developmental states put economic growth—rather than equality, welfare, democracy, or human rights—as their top priority. Subsequently, economic growth (GNPism) and nationalism became the twin bases of legitimacy for the East Asian developmental states. Because of its emphasis on the bureaucrats' technical expertise, the state's literature often forgets that East Asian developmental states were a historical product of the Cold War and nationalism.

Why the Developmental State Became the Main Agent? A distinguished feature of East Asian developmental states is that they have a strong state but a weak capitalist class (and a weak society). Since no other agent in the society could take the lead, the strong state has become the main agent by default. But what explains the existence of a strong state in East Asia in the first place?

In this respect, the Cold War has laid the foundation of strong East Asian developmental state. Needless to stress, East Asian states were much weakened after going through long-years of fighting and subsequent defeat during World War II. The reason why East Asian states could quickly rebuild themselves after the war was mostly a result of the anti-communist policy of the U.S. In order to turn Japan, South Korea, and Taiwan as bulwarks against communism, the U.S. not just provided them with military aids, tolerated their authoritarian policies, and supported their military regimes, but also injected a large amount of economic aids and offered them lucrative American contracts. The arrival of American industrial orders needed for the Korea War in the early 1950s, for example, helped to lift the Japanese economy out of recession and put it on a course of rapid growth. In South Korea and Taiwan, foreign economic assistance in the 1950s figured heavily in alleviating huge government budget deficits, financing investment, and paying for imports.

With influx of massive U.S. aids and contracts, the East Asian states were empowered to develop their market economies. As they faced keen global competition in the era of late industrialization, they could afford no time for their small capitalist class to mature, to acquire entrepreneurial skills, and to be brave enough to invest in risky industries. Thus, the developmental states had to take a more "catalytic" role to hatch the capitalists, to govern the market and to promote the economy.

Why State Intervention Worked? The Cold War has also provided a breathing space for the developmental states to try out their economic policies. In other countries in the South, since transnational corporations already gain a foothold in their domestic economies, it is hard for any domestic corporation to build up strength to compete with the transnational corporations. Cheap, high quality foreign imports easily destroyed domestic products. However, in East Asia due to the Cold War situation, the U.S. was willing to institute a peculiar arrangement that was contrary to the interests of American corporations. The East Asian Cold War allies of the U.S. were allowed to close their markets to American imports in order to strengthen their domestic industries. And when their industrial products were competitive enough to be sold to the world economy, the U.S. generously opened her American market in order to push East Asian states to promote export-led industrialization. The U.S. market was critical to the growth of East Asia states, because it was their largest single market throughout the 1960s and 1970s. This geopolitical strategy of the U.S. during the Cold War, therefore, explains why, despite the notorious closed domestic markets of South Korea and Taiwan, their exports could still enjoy unrestricted access to the American market for so long.

Because of this American open-door policy, the East Asian developmental states worked hard on export-led industrialization to capture this competitive market. The developmental state provided incentives such as bank loans, subsidizes, technical assistance, and tax incentives to encourage exports. However, because the export market is highly competitive, the developmental states also disciplined their domestic corporations if they failed to meet the stringent export requirements. Thus, Amsden[4] asserts that where Korea differs from other late industrializing countries is in the discipline its state exercises over private firms.

What is the Dark Side of Developmental States? Finally, the Cold War had endorsed the authoritarianism of East Asian developmental states. In the name of anti-communism, East Asian military regimes were permitted to stay in power, and they were allowed to impose martial law onto the civil society. Subsequently, in East Asian developmental states, strikes were banned, existing unions were outlawed, newspapers were censored, and movement activists were arrested. Labour subordination was an important mean to make workers docile, to make their wages low, and to make them work long hours, otherwise the exports of the East Asian developmental states would not be so cheap and competitive in the global market. In highlighting the technical nature of developmental states, the statist literature seldom discusses its dark side.

As a historical product of the Cold War, the developmental state would lose many of its distinguished features when the Cold War ends. In this case, we observe that many East Asian developmental states in the 1990s were attacked by a variety of different social forces: transnational corporations wanted to use such global agency as the WTO to open their internal markets; human rightists and democrats challenged their authoritarian policy; labour unions, women leaders, and other movement activists wanted higher wages, more welfare, and the expansion of gender and ethnic equalities.

In sum, although the statist literature has contributed to our understanding of the decisive role of the state in development, it is necessary to go beyond the narrow focus on the expertise and planning of the bureaucrats in order to understand the origins, characteristics, and dynamics of East Asian developmental states. This paper argues that the Cold War and U.S. hegemonic struggles had provided the urgency of national development, the resources, the golden market opportunities, and the authoritarianism of East Asian developmental states.

This Cold War focus helps us understand the trajectory of the Chinese state in the post war era, as the development of the Chinese communist state is the mirror image of the formation of East Asian developmental states. It is a pity that the statist literature has neglected the study of the Chinese communist state. As this paper argues in the following section, the Chinese communist state has undergone structural mutation since 1978 and is now acting like an East Asian developmental state.

3. The Maoist Revolutionary State in Communist China

At first glance, the Chinese communist state during the Maoist era (1949-1976) is totally different from East Asian development states. While East Asian developmental states put economic growth as their top priority, the Chinese communist state put egalitarianism as its number one goal and wanted to eliminate exploitation and class domination. Maoism stressed equality, selflessness, collectivism, and serving the people. At the height of the Cultural Revolution, not only the new middle class and capitalists but also the party officials "who were carrying the capitalist road" were attacked. Intellectuals and party officials were sent to the countryside to do "labour" so as to be educated by poor peasants.

In addition, although East Asian developmental states were successful in raising economic growth and living standard, the Chinese communist state had failed to do so. China's per capita annual income was still less than US$530 in the 1970s, due to the extraordinary growth of her population from around 500 million in 1953 to around 1 billion in 1980. Despite the fact that over 70 percent of the total workforce were deployed in agriculture and the adoption of a "grain first" policy, China could not produce enough food to sustain a barest level of consumption for the population. Thus, communist China still ranked among the poorest nations in the world, and her standard of living remained very low.

Nevertheless, despite the Chinese communist state put eqalitarianism as the top priority and failed to attain economic growth, it did share some structural similarities with East Asian developmental states and thus had laid the foundation for the metamorphosis into the latter at the turn of the twenty-first century.

First, the Cold War had induced a strong communist party-state in China, because China's political order had to be strengthened to confront the "imperialist enemies" without (notably during the Korean War) and the "counter-revolutionaries" (notably the remnants of the Nationalist Party opposition) within. Due to the fusion of functions and the overlapping of personnel among the communist party, the state bureaucracy, and the army, there was an excess concentration of power in the vanguard Leninist party. Only political organizations (like peasants' associations, labour unions, and women's associations) formally sponsored by the Party were allowed to operate; other organizations were either made ineffective or simply banned from operation.

This Leninist party-state was all-powerful in the sense that it extended both vertically and horizontally to every sphere in the Chinese society. Vertically, the Leninist party-state was the first Chinese government that was able to exert its political control all the way down to village, family, and individual levels. Horizontally, there was a great expansion of state functions. The Leninist state did not just collect tax and keep social order, but also oversaw such functions as education, health care, marriage, culture, and carried out such economic policies and political movements as the land reform, collectivization, the Great Leap Forward, and the Cultural Revolution. In this respect, the Chinese communist state had even more state autonomy and more state capacity than its counterparts in East Asian NIEs.

Second, another overlooked fact is that the Cold War had

induced a strong dose of nationalism in Chinese society. If East Asian NIEs (like South Korea and Taiwan) faced the threat of national survival from their communist rivals, their communist rivals too had faced similar threat from the U.S. and its capitalist allies. During the Cold War, the U.S. sent warships to patrol the Taiwan Strait and supported the defeated Nationalist Party in Taiwan, sent soldiers to fight against the communists in Korea, supported counter-revolutionary activities in China, froze Chinese assets in the United States, imposed an economic embargo on Chinese products, prevented China from gaining a seat in the United Nations, and waged ideological attacks on Chinese and Soviet "communist totalitarianism" in the mass media.

Intense hostility from the U.S. served to preclude certain developmental options for the nascent Chinese communist state. Cut off from contacts with capitalist core states, the Chinese state could not possibly pursue export-oriented industrialization (due to the closure of Western markets) or import-substitution (due to the economic embargo). The Chinese communist state eventually relied upon national instead of external resources and put forward an indigenous "self-reliance" model of development, stressing national autonomy, pride in being a poor country, and mass mobilization.

Thus, although the Chinese communist state was not developmental in orientation, it was highly nationalist. Like other East Asian developmental states, the Chinese communist state wanted to be rich and powerful. In this respect, the Chinese communist state had possessed some key ingredients of the developmental states, i.e., a strong state with autonomy and capacity, and the nationalistic urge to be strong and powerful. In addition, the Maoist legacy also provided the following facilitating conditions for the structural mutation into a developmental state.

Third, the Maoist legacy provided the much-needed rural

infrastructure and local institutions for the success of a developmental state. It was during the Maoist era that reservoirs were constructed, irrigation system strengthened, and drainage network improved. During the Great Leap Forward, the state mobilized millions of peasants to construct dams, reservoirs, and large-scale irrigation systems for the communes. It was also during the Maoist era that rural industries and enterprises were set up in the communes, local officials accumulated managerial experience through running commune and brigade enterprises, and local governments were asked to promote development in the community. The Maoist commune model and its decentralization policy provided the medium to tap local resources, to train local leaders, and to arouse local initiatives. Without all these infrastructure and institutional foundations built in the Maoist era, rural reform and local village and township enterprises could not have started so easily and so fast in the 1980s.

Finally, the Chinese communist state incurred almost no foreign debt. In stark contrast to Eastern European states and Russia, the Chinese state need not devote huge resources to service foreign debt, nor China need to resort to crushing bailout packages by the International Monetary Fund to shore up its economic reforms in the 1980s.

In sum, the Maoist era has provided many favourable legacies, structures, and conditions for the metamorphosis of the communist state into a developmental state. Still, like other state elites, communist state officials wanted to keep their status quo rather than moving into an uncertain future. Most communist states had, in fact, experienced breakdown and were overthrown before they agreed to transform themselves into some other forms.

4. The Critical Transition to Developmentalism

During the Maoist era, some bureaucratic elites did try to steer the Chinese communist state toward the development of productive force during the mid 1950s, the early 1960s, and the early 1970s. But their efforts resulted in complete failure. They were branded as "capitalist roaders" and purged. Only in the late 1970s did they succeed. As such, what explains the critical transition from a revolutionary communist state to a developmental state in China?

This paper argues that China's critical transition to developmentalism is the product of the following factors: the fading of the Cold War, East Asian industrial relocation, Chinese diaspora capitalism, and several triggering events.

The Fading of the Cold War : If the Cold War prevented the Chinese communist state from pursuing either export-oriented industrialization or import substitution in the capitalist world economy, the fading of the Cold War since the 1970s had provided the pre-condition for the Chinese state to re-enter the world-economy to pursue developmental objectives.

The late 1970s was a period of declining American hegemony. Economically, the U.S. faced the problems of inflation, low productivity, and recession. Its products were under strong competition with Japanese and German manufactures in the world market. Politically, the U.S. was still plagued by its defeat in Vietnam and its failed attempt to fend off global Soviet expansionism. At this historical conjuncture, the U.S. welcomed China back to the world-economy. China could be a new regional power to counterbalance Soviet military expansion and Japanese economic expansion in East Asia. Moreover, the vast Chinese market, cheap Chinese labour, and abundant Chinese raw materials and minerals could considerably increase the competitive power of American industry in the world market.

In addition, the fading of the Cold War was accompanied by the disillusion of the socialist path of development. By the end of the 1970s, the economies of the socialist states in Eastern Europe were in disarray, haunted by foreign debts, low growth rates, and declining living standards. This failure further convinced the Chinese state that it was necessary to bring developmentalism back in order to rejuvenate the stagnant Chinese economy.

While disillusioned with its former socialist allies, the Chinese state was impressed with the economic success of its East Asian neighbors.

East Asian Industrial Relocation: With U.S. support in the 1950s and the 1960s, Japan, South Korea, Taiwan, and Hong Kong had become highly industrialized and their people enjoyed a much higher living standard than that in China. Thus, the Chinese state was motivated to follow the path of its successful East Asian neighbours to engage in export-oriented industrialization.

Furthermore, as Hong Kong, Taiwan, and South Korea were upgraded to the status of NIEs in the late 1970s, they gradually lost their geopolitical privileges with the U.S. They, too, had to face the trade restrictions (tariffs, quota, rising foreign currency value). Due to their economic success, there were also labour shortages, increasing labour disputes, escalating land prices, and the emergence of environmental protests—all of which served to raise the cost of production in the East Asian NIEs. As a result, the Asian NIEs felt the need of promoting an industrial relocation in order to secure a stable supply of cheap, docile labor force, and other resources in the 1980s.

Industrial relocation of the NIEs provided a strong incentive for the Chinese state to promote developmental objectives. From the Chinese perspective, China could be a favourable site for the NIEs' relocation because it has abundant cheap labour, land, and other resources. China was also quite close to Hong Kong, Taiwan, and South Korea, and they share a common Confucian cultural heritage. Therefore, the Chinese state set up four special economic zones (SEZs) in 1979, opened fourteen coastal cities and Hainan Island in 1984 and three delta areas in 1985 for foreign investment, and pursued a coastal developmental strategy to enhance export industrialization in 1988.

Chinese Diaspora Capitalism: During the Cold War era, the influx of U.S. aids, loans, and contracts greatly helped East Asian states to solve the problem of primitive accumulation and had greatly enhanced their states' capacity to promote developmental policies. The U.S., of course, would not provide similar aids, loans, and contracts to the Chinese state to assist its developmental programs after the fading of the Cold War.

Fortunately, there was a comparable influx of capital in the form of Chinese diaspora investment to China at the initial phase of transition to provide capital for primitive accumulation. Before 1978, Chinese diaspora capitalism thrived in Hong Kong, Taiwan, Singapore, and overseas Chinese communities. After the Chinese state adopted an open door policy for foreign investment, Hong Kong accounted for the bulk of China's foreign investment and foreign trade. In the early 1990s, Hong Kong firms employed over 3 million workers in the Pearl River Delta. By the end of the 1980s, Taiwan became the second largest trading partner and investor for Mainland China. In the 1990s, overseas Chinese entrepreneurs in Southeast Asia have shown a visible interest in conducting trade and investment in China.

Diaspora capitalists from Hong Kong and Taiwan have been very active in South China because this was the region in which most overseas Chinese came from. Diaspora capitalists drew upon pre-existing social connections—such as shared experiences and qualities as being classmates, colleagues, common native place, and kinship—to facilitate their business transactions. The earliest diaspora capitalists utilized their own kin connections in their native towns and villages. Later diaspora capitalists, however, have frequently been introduced to an investment site through the recommendation of friends who have previously established production there. Once social connections (guanxi) are established with the South China side, they can be used to gain introduction to local officials, to circumvent bureaucratic inefficiencies, and to solve problems of material shortages[5].

Even though the fading of the Cold War had provided the preconditions, the East Asian industrial relocation had provided the incentive, and Chinese diaspora capitalism had provided the capital for primitive accumulation for the transformation to a developmental state, it still requires several triggering events to overcome the inertia of the communist status quo.

Triggering Events : Yimin Lin[6] points out that the critical event that set in motion the efforts to reform the economic system was the passing of the old generation of revolutionary leaders. The death of Mao in 1976 was followed by the rise of a new coalition of political leaders who were leaning or receptive to some form of economic institutional change. Most of them were victims of the Cultural Revolution. Their return was accompanied by a national rehabilitation of lower level party-state functionaries. Most of these functionaries had prior experience in formulating and implementing economic policies.

Yimin Lin[7] further explains that the shift in policy focus from socialist egalitarianism to economic developmentalism and the reshuffling of local leaders opened way for bottom-up institutional innovation. In provinces like Anhui, pro-reform leaders gave tolerance and even encouragement to certain attempts made by grassroots officials. This significantly changed the political risk perceived by the rank-and-file of the local state apparatus. Subsequently, when severe national disasters hit during 1977-79, some local officials resorted to various form of family production and justified their rule breaking on the ground of coping with natural disaster. The good results of family farming in turn provided a ground of justification for the arrangement to be introduced to other provinces, which later led to decollectivization and the institutionalization of Household Responsibility system in the countryside.

In short, the fading of the Cold War, East Asian industrial relocation, Chinese diaspora capitalism, and triggering events had promoted the Chinese state to cross the communist divide and engaged in developmental policies. In a short span of two decades since 1978, the Chinese state quickly transformed itself to a developmental state.

5. The Formation of the Chinese Developmental State

The Chinese state has exhibited the following features of a developmental state: having a strong state machinery, engaging in "reform from above", controlling the sequence of reforms, actively intervening in local economy, is highly nationalistic, and attaining high rate of economic growth.

Reform from Above : Because of the Leninist state legacy, the Chinese state had the strength to adopt the "reform from above" strategy. Even though the Chinese state faced many developmental problems in the mid 1970s, its situation was not desperate. The Chinese state was not under any threat of foreign invasion, economic bankruptcy, or rebellion from below. As such, the Chinese state still had the autonomy and capacity to propose and implement various developmental policies under its control. The state could select certain types of developmental policies, could vary the speed of reform, and, most importantly, had the freedom of making corrections to its mistakes.

Therefore, different from the "one bang" approach in Eastern Europe, the developmental policies in China have been a gradual, adaptive process without a clear blueprint. John McMillan and Barry Naughton[8] remark: the reforms have proceeded by trial and error, with frequent mid-course corrections and reversals of policy. In other words, the Chinese developmental policies were not a complete project settled in the first stage, but an ongoing process with many adjustments. There was no rapid leap to free prices, currency convertibility, or cutting of state subsidies; nor there was massive privatization and the quick selling off of state enterprises. This gradualist approach practiced by the Chinese state was quite different to those "one bang" and "shock therapy" approaches practiced in Eastern Europe, which called for the dismantling of centrally planned economy as soon as possible. As Andrew Walder[9] remarks, "Where in Europe shock therapy and mass privatization are designed in part to dismantle Communism and strip former Communists of power and privilege, in China gradual reform is intended to allow the Party to survive as an instrument of economic development."

Reform Sequence: The Chinese state benefited from carrying out reforms in the countryside before proposing any reform on urban economy. Rural reforms were much less complicated than urban reforms. In the late 1970s, the Chinese state increased procurement prices for agricultural products, encouraged peasants to engage in cash crop and rural industrial production, and allowed peasants to work in nearby market towns and faraway cities. After the rural reforms succeeded, the Chinese state was more confident to work on the complicated urban reforms in the 1980s. Rising agricultural productivity, in turn, released surplus labour from the countryside, providing a large number of cheap labourers to urban factories.

Furthermore, in the Soviet Union, political reforms were carried out before economic reforms, with the hope that democratization would provide the communist party-state with the needed support to overcome bureaucratic resistance toward economic reforms. The Soviet state also carried out reforms in urban areas first because of the deep-rooted problems in the countryside. However, political reforms had unintentionally released new political forces that opposed the communist party, and urban unrest eventually led to the overthrow of the communist state in the Soviet Union.

In contrast, the Chinese state promoted economic reforms before carrying out major democratic reforms. In the late 1970s, communes were dismantled and peasants were asked to be responsible for their own living. In the early 1980s, the Chinese state tried to promote enterprise reforms to increase the power of the managers. In the mid 1980s, the Chinese state further opened fourteen coastal cities to attract foreign investment. Although in the reform period the Chinese state showed more tolerance toward dissent, granted more freedom toward its citizen, and allowed local elections at the village level, the Chinese state was reluctant to promote any serious democratic reform to allow multi-party elections at the provincial and national level. As a result, the Chinese state could retain the Leninist structure. Not only it needed not share power with other political parties, it also needed not worry about the critical democratic voices in the civil society and the uncertainty of election outcomes. Without being distracted by democratic reforms, the Chinese state was able to concentrate on the economic front to promote its developmental programs.

Decentralization and Local Development : Attracted by the policy of fiscal decentralization through which local states could keep part of the tax revenue, local leaders quickly engaged in market activities. The result was the formation of township and village enterprises (TVEs), which were not bound by the central plan and were free to seek out market opportunities. Kyung-Sup Chang[10] remarks that on the part of local states, running rural industries is no new experience since they had been in charge of rural industries since the Great Leap Forward in the late 1950s. Seizing the golden opportunity created by the policy of fiscal decentralization, local states have created a favorable political and administrative environment for new industrial ventures, renovate or build factories, set up corporate organizations, mobilize villagers' economic resources, secure financial and technical cooperation from urban enterprises, and staff the management of rural industrial enterprises.

Focusing on the South China case, George Lin[11] further points out that a new "bottom up" development mechanism is taking shape in which initiatives are made primarily by local states to solicit overseas Chinese and domestic capital, mobilize labour and land resources, and lead the local economy to enter the orbit of international division of labour and global competition. Drawing upon Guangdong's Dongguan County as a case study, George Lin[12] shows that this local state has sought every possible opportunity to cultivate kinship ties and interpersonal trusts with the diaspora capitalists in Hong Kong in order to attract them to invest in Dongguan county. Special policies, including taxation concessions and preferential treatment regarding the import of necessary equipment and the handling of foreign currency, were announced to attract foreign investment. A special office was set up by the local Chinese state to serve Hong Kong investors with efficient personnel and simplified bureaucratic procedures. Economic cooperation between Dongguan and Hong Kong was arranged creatively and flexibly in a variety of forms, including joint ventures, cooperative ventures, export processing, and compensation trade. The general pattern is that designing and marketing are handled in Hong Kong, while labour intensive processes are performed in Dongguan.

Strong Economic Growth : As a result of the above developmental policies, economic growth in China in the same period was nothing but spectacular. The average annual growth rate of real gross domestic product (GDP) was 9 percent between 1978-1994 and 10.7 percent between 1990-1999. Even in the aftermath of the Asian financial crisis, China still recorded an 8 percent GDP growth rate in 2000 and a projected 7.3 percent GDP growth rate in 2001. If such impressive economic growth rates continue, China could be transformed into the world's second largest economy in a decade or so. The real GDP grew from 681 billion yuan in 1978 to 8,190 billion yuan in 1999; Chinese per capita income rose from 316 yuan in 1978 to 6,456 yuan in 1999. China recorded a trade surplus of almost US$44 billion in 1998, a current account surplus (about 1 percent of

GDP in 1996 but close to 3 percent in 1997), and held a very large foreign exchange reserve of US$ 200 billion in 1999[13]. In this respect, the Chinese state has made it to a Newly Industrializing Economies like the other East Asian NIEs.

Nationalism : Finally, the Chinese state also exhibits a strong dose of nationalism like the East Asian NIEs. Suzanne Odgen[14] explains that the Chinese state is now confronting the problem of how to fill the void created by the collapse of communitarian values fostered by Marxism-Leninism-Mao Zedong Thought. Furthermore, the Chinese state is facing the divisive and destabilizing forces of capitalism, individualism, commercialism, and modernization, forces that have undercut the sense of community in China. The search for communitarian values to replace those of communism has led to official support for the values of nationalism, patriotism, and the reinvention of Chinese popular culture. In particular, the Chinese state tried to revive Chinese culture as part of an effort to confront a "fever" for Western ideas. Its overall goal was to use culture to bolster the power of (cultural) nationalism. Also, to be a "patriot" in today's China means to support the national community and its goals, notably, national reunification, economic growth, and political stability.

Suzanne Odgen argues that the Chinese people have embraced cultural nationalism and patriotism with passion, as shown by the fact that even Chinese dissidents have overwhelmingly taken the government's side in defending the Chinese state's claims to Taiwan and Tibet, their extraordinary pleasure in Hong Kong's return to Beijing rule in 1997, and their anger at what they interpret as the West's support for Japan's military expansion and containment of China, including U.S. consideration of plans to build a "theatre missile defense" in Northeast Asia that would protect Japan, and possibly Taiwan, from attack.

In sum, the Chinese state has been transformed into a

developmental state over the past two decades. It has put economic growth as its top priority. It has a strong state institution to impose reforms from the above, to control the sequence of the reforms, and to arouse developmental initiatives from the local states. Its developmental policies now bear fruit and the Chinese economy is expanding very rapidly. By the 1990s, economic growth and nationalism have become the twin bases of legitimacy for the Chinese developmental state.

Nevertheless, due to its communist origins, the Chinese developmental state has faced the following problems of socialist transition: The implementation of economic reforms, the embourgeoisiement of cadres, and emergent social conflict.

6. The Problems of Socialist Transition

The Implementation of Economic Reforms : In other East Asian states, their task was to expand and strengthen the state sector and state regulations, so they had more resources and rules to plan the economy and govern the market. In China, the situation was completely different. Due to the legacy of a planned economy, the state sector in China was already overwhelming. The task for the Chinese developmental state, therefore, was to cut down the state sector, expand the capitalist sector, and inject entrepreneurship into the economy.

In the financial sector, for instance, Carsten Holz and Tian Zhu[15] explain that the Chinese state is facing three financial crises: bad loans in the state banks, losses in the state-owned enterprises (SOEs), and government budget deficits. By the mid-1990s, estimates of the state banks' bad loans ranged from 20 percent to about 50 points. Moreover, losses of industrial SOEs increased drastically in the late 1980s and continued to rise through the late 1990s. The ratio of profit of profitable enterprises to the losses of loss-making enterprises after 1985 fell to an all-time low in 1997. Third, with regard to government budget deficits, the fiscal balance deteriorated from a small budget surplus in 1978 to a deficit equivalent to more than 10 percent of expenditures in 1990s. In 2000, the budget deficit was equivalent to 4.55 percent of GDP.

Holz and Zhu further stress that these three financial crises are intricately linked. For example, social security payments could be made either by SOEs or through the government budget. If they are made by an SOE, they reduce SOE profit; if they are financed through government budget, they increase the government budget deficit. Infrastructure projects could either be financed through government budget appropriations, increasing the government budget deficit, or through state-ordained low-interest loans from the state banks, reducing bank profits. In this respect, reforming one sector (either the bank, the SOE, or the government budget) without reforming the other two will not have an effective outcome. The extent of banks' bad loans, SOE losses, and government fiscal shortfalls reflect more than a political decision on where within the state sector to place the financial deficit attributable only to the state sector as a whole.

Up to now, these financial crises have been ameliorated by the Chinese state's rapid economic development. However, once China's high-speed economic growth slows down, the problem of bad loans, SOE losses, and government deficit will become explosive.

The Embourgeoisiement of Cadres: Although East Asian developmental state officials targeted industry, provided incentives, and monitored corporate performance, they seldom directly engaged in running the companies themselves. In China, however, state officials and private capitalists are often the same persons.

Since the old Chinese capitalist class was eliminated in the 1950s, a new class of capitalist entrepreneurs has to be created in order to promote marketization reforms. During the first decade of the economic reforms which aimed to create a private sector, cadres turned local state and collective enterprises into profitable township enterprises (local state corporatism), developed joint ventures with foreign capitalists and overseas Chinese capitalists, quit their official positions and set up their own capitalist enterprises, and hired their kin and friends to run them. Since cadres possessed political capital as well as the necessary networks to run their enterprises, they had an edge over other classes in taking advantages of the nascent business opportunities[16].

During the second stage of reform in the 1990s, when the state called for privatization and "Grasp the big, release the small," there is a massive diversion of the assets and profits of state enterprises into the private hands of the cadres in charge of them[17]. Ding's[18] studies point to the following ways that state enterprises can be stripped of. In Organizational proliferation, cadres stripped off its best-equipped or most profitable segments and turn these into new collective-owned companies. "One manager, two businesses" happens when cadres established their own private business by usurping assets from the state industries in which they hold executive positions. Francis[19] points out that these practices are carried out by all sorts of state entities: "local and municipal governments, national ministries, the army, national and local public security bureaus, party organizations, universities, scientific institutes." The coexistence and inter-penetration of various forms of ownerships between the state and the non-state domain have provided a golden opportunity for cadres to transform themselves capitalist owners and managers of semi-state, collective, and private properties.

The fuzzy property boundaries and the mutation between state managers and capitalists have created an all-powerful hybrid which can be called a "cadre-capitalist" class. Goodman[20] reports that "most entrepreneurs, including those in the private sector of the economy... either had social origins in the party-state or were for the most part incorporated into its activities." This hybrid state-capitalist class has monopolized political capital, economic capital, and social/network capital in the Chinese society. Its members are the beneficiaries of the existing arrangements of partial reforms, mixed economy, and hybrid ownership.

In Russia and Eastern Europe, former state officials also engaged in stripping the assets of state enterprises. However, although such activity in Russia and Eastern Europe had led to rent seeking and the decline of their economies, state officials in China sometimes invested in productive, profitable enterprises because both the domestic market and the global markets are highly competitive. The critical issue, then, is how to induce Chinese state-capitalists to move from rent seeking to productive economic activities.

Class Conflict : Although the Chinese state has been successful in incorporating new social forces and suppressing democratic reforms, these political issues will become more explosive once they are combined with the economic issues of enterprise bankruptcy, unemployment, and global recession.

Kam Wing Chan[21] estimates that about 10 million workers are expected to be laid off in the state sector in the next five years, and layoffs carry the risk of triggering urban political turmoil. In addition, despite a massive outflow of rural migrant workers, 90 million laborers in the countryside need jobs. The sluggish performance of the urban economy, job competition from laid-off workers in the state sector, and increasingly protectionist policies by the local states against the migrant workers will make it harder and harder for them to find jobs in the cities. A large "floating population" could easily become the source of social conflict.

Kyung-Sup Chang[22] further laments that even when migrant workers have found employment, they have to endure all kinds of social and economic hardships because of the constraints imposed upon them by the old household registration system. For example, it is extremely difficult, if not impossible, for migrant workers to acquire social services (such as education and health care for their children), while such services are offered to regular urban residents as a sort of citizenship rights.

At the same time, wealth gap is growing very rapidly. According to a World Bank report in 1997, the Gini Coefficient (an international measurement of income disparity) rose from 0.28 in the 1989s to a dangerously high 0.43 in 2000. The richest 20 percent of Beijing people owned 11 times as much in assets as the poorest 20 percent. Subsequently, there could be a serious possibility that grassroots people's frustration and resistance are expressed not only against richer neighbors but also much more crucially against the state and its local agents. The numerous stories about corruption, favoritism, abuses of power, and extravagant life styles of cadres reported in the Chinese newspapers and magazines are an expression of this grassroots frustration. In this context, state authority can easily be identified with economic injustice. Such grassroots sentiment could express itself in strikes, street demonstrations, social movements, and riots across the country. Kyung-Sup Chang reports that over the past few years peasants in many inland provinces rioted against corrupt and extorting local cadres, and in many big cities unemployed and impoverished groups have staged rallies against their local governments for their economic mishaps. Even anti-corruption campaigns can be seen as a form of class politics catering to the desire of grassroots peasants, workers, and migrants.

Since the Chinese state is still supposedly upholding the communist ideology that workers and peasants are the masters of society, and since the old grassroots generation perceived job, housing, welfare, pension and health care services as their entitlements, it would be difficult for the Chinese state to justify its firing of workers and taking away of the workers' housing, welfare, and health care rights. To do so, the Chinese state would risk public demonstration and social conflict in the society.

7. The Problems of Reintegration into the Capitalist World-Economy

Aside from the problems of socialist transition, the Chinese developmental state also faced the problems of reintegration of China into the capitalist world economy, i.e., the challenge of hegemonic rivalry with the U.S. and the challenge from globalization forces.

The Challenge of Hegemonic Rivalry: Because of China's communist legacy, the Bush administration tends to perceive China as a strategic competitor. The rapid economic development of China over the past two decades has also made the U.S. worry that the Chinese state could challenge its global hegemony in the future.

Suzanne Odgen[23] points to the following ways that the U.S. has exerted its influence over China in hegemonic struggles:

- Since 1989, the U.S. has used the human rights as a pretext to threaten the end of China's most-favored-nation trade status (normal trade status), has denied China the right to host the year 2000 Olympics, and has blocked China's entry into the World Trade Organization for years;
- The U.S. has accused China of stealing nuclear secrets and making illegal contributions to the U.S. Democratic Party in the 1996 elections;
- The U.S. continued to support Taiwan's military and had sent two U.S. aircraft carrier battle units to Taiwan in 1996;
- The U.S. bombed the Chinese Embassy in Belgrade in May 1999 during the war over Kosovo;
- The U.S. carried out air surveillance of China, which precipitated the crash of a Chinese jet, the death of its pilot, and an emergency landing of the U.S. plane on the island of Hainan;

- The U.S. decided to build a theatre missile defence system that might include Taiwan, as well as to build a national U.S. defence that would deny China a second strike capability.

Although the war against terrorism in late 2001 has temporarily overshadowed the hegemonic rivalry between the U.S. and China, it is too early to tell whether such rivalry could be rekindled when the war against terrorism ends.

The Challenge of Globalization: Another crucial question is whether the Chinese state's rapid economic development can continue and for how long. During the Asian financial crisis in the late 1990s, China's foreign investment and exports experienced a slight decline. Only after the Asian financial crisis had passed away did China receive the former level of foreign investment and exports. However, at the beginning of the twenty-first century, both the U.S. and Japan have moved into economic recession. If a global economic recession continues for a fairly long period, it could produce a dampening effect on the Chinese economy, leading to a decline of foreign investment and exports, a rapid rise of unemployment, new pressures to devaluate the Chinese currency, etc.

Furthermore, Globalization through WTO accession is likely to produce significant competitive pressures on the agriculture sector. Kam Wing Chan[24] (2000) estimates that China will lose about 3 million jobs in agriculture due to the competition of imported farm products. Another report quoting government sources said 20 million rural jobs would be lost because of China's WTO entry. In the urban sector, many old and less competitive industries and enterprises would lose out in the short term after WTO entry. In this respect, the problem of job loses and unemployment will become the top agenda of the Chinese state in the first decade of the twenty-first century.

WTO accession may have a negative impact on China's telecommunications, automobile, and banking industries as well. For example, the Asian Development Bank points out that China's banking sector, one of the most protected in the world, is particularly vulnerable. In the short to medium term, local bank's net interest margins will narrow and profitability will be squeezed. To face the challenges from international banks after WTO accession, reform of the finance sector must be accelerated. The key problem is to tackle the problem of non-performing loans and to establish an effective corporate governance system.

Furthermore, China was less affected by the Asian financial crisis in the late 1990s because its currency was not convertible and it had strong control over the banking sector and foreign trade, and because the Chinese economy drew greatly on domestic markets and was less exposed to international market fluctuations than many of its neighbors. However, WTO entry will increase China's global economic integration. Any global recession in the early twenty-first century would exert a more serious impact on the Chinese economy than before.

8. Conclusion

Similarities with East Asian Developmental States: From the above discussion, it is obvious that the Chinese development state has shared many similar characteristics with its East Asian counterpart. *First,* they have an autonomous state that had the capacity to formulate and implement developmental policies. In China, since the strong Leninist party-state remained largely intact in the post-1978 reform era, the Chinese state had the capacity to introduce certain types of economic programs, to vary the speed and the sequence of reform, and to make corrections or even reverse its policies if necessary.

Second, the developmental states adopted authoritarian policies to deactivate civil society, discipline labor, and suppress dissent in order to maintain a favorable environment to attract foreign and domestic investment and to maintain political stability. In China, the legacy of the Leninist party-state and corporatism helped the Chinese state to deal with the emerging social forces unleashed by economic reforms.

Third, since the developmental states did not carry out any democratic reforms but relied upon suppression and corporatism for political control, they needed a different basis of legitimacy from that of the Western democratic states. In China, like other East Asian developmental states, the basis of legitimacy was mainly derived from "GNPism" and nationalism. The claims were that citizens should support the state because their incomes had greatly improved, their living standards were much better than that of the older generation, and they should unite behind the state in order to create a rich and powerful nation free of domination from the foreigners.

The China Difference: Despite the above similarities, the Chinese developmental state is different from its East Asian counterparts in the following ways. First, the Chinese developmental state has exhibited a strong tendency toward entrepreneurship. Although East Asian developmental state officials are promoting the hatching of capitalists, they seldom turn themselves into capitalists and involve in running the corporations. In China, however, not only were state officials asked to be good managers and turned state enterprises into profit-making businesses, but many state officials also informally turned public assets into quasi-public, quasi-private properties, or simply into private companies. As it is well documented in the China field, there is a fuzzy boundary between state enterprises and collective/private enterprises, and it is difficult to draw a clear boundary between state officials and private capitalists in China. Rather, the Chinese characteristic is a hybrid "state-capitalist" walking on two legs in both the state sector and the private sector.

Second, the Chinese development state has exhibited a pattern of local, "bottom-up" strategy. East Asian developmental states had adopted a centralized policy, and it was their central governments that played the most active role in development. However, in China, due to the legacy of communism, the present policy of fiscal decentralization, and the vast territory of China, local officials in provincial, county, and village governments had played a much more active role than their counterparts in East Asian developmental states. Instead of promoting the development of urban industrialization and mega cities, Chinese local state officials have promoted the development of rural industrialization and small and medium cities. This pattern of dispersed development will have a profound impact on China in the future.

Third, although the Chinese development state has relied on "GNPism" and nationalism as its bases of legitimacy, it had also paid more attention to egalitarianism than its East Asian counterparts during their industrial take-off phase. Having gone through the legacy of revolutionary socialism under the Maoist regime, and having the constitution still written that workers and peasants are the masters of society, the Chinese "developmental" state was much more vulnerable to the charges of inequality, poverty, and exploitation than its East Asian development states counterparts. Thus, the Chinese state had many times backed off from carrying out those policies that could lead to massive layoffs and the elimination of social safety nets.

Prospects: If the Chinese state fails to implement economic reforms, if the accession to WTO brings more harms than benefits to the China, if the global economic recession is long and serious, and if the U.S. sees China more as a strategic competitor than as a strategic partner, then the prospect for the Chinese developmental state may be threatened.

However, two decades of generally uninterrupted economic growth have greatly strengthened the Chinese economy, providing a breathing space for the Chinese developmental state to try all sorts of policies to deal with the problems of enterprise reforms and banking reforms. For example, the Chinese state in 2002 proposed to boost the economy by investing in infrastructure projects, developing western provinces, upgrading technology for state-owned enterprises, education, and a project to transport water from the Yangtze River to northern provinces. Massive state investments, China's abundant reserves (materials, food, and foreign exchange), and huge domestic market should help China to meet the challenges of development. Thus, the Chinese developmental state should have the experience to handle the challenges of WTO accession and global market fluctuation, while China's vast domestic economy should be able to provide an economic powerhouse for the economic growth to continue. Economic growth in turn would enhance the state's capacity to solve the emerging social conflict in society, so Chinese Communist Party could hold onto power for a longer time.

However, history never follows a pre-determined path but is always subject to the intervention of human agency. The prospect for the China's development, therefore, depends very much on how the Chinese developmental state handles the problems of socialist transition and the problems of reintegration into the world-economy.

Notes and References

1. Chalmers Johnson, *MITI and the Japanese Miracle,* Stanford University Press, 1982; and Alice Amsden, *Asia's Next Giant : South Korea and Late Industrialization,* New York : Oxford University Press, 1989.
2. Wally Goldfrank, "Review of Chalmers Johnson's MITI and the Japanese Miracle", *Contemporary Sociology* 12, 1983, 722-723; and John Lie, "Review : Rethinking the 'Miracle' — Economic Growth and Political Struggles in South Korea", *Bulletin of Concerned Asian Scholars,* 23 (4), 1991, 66-71.
3. Meredith Woo-Cumings, "Introduction : Chalmers Johnson

and the Politics of Nationalism and Development", Meredith Woo-Cumings (ed.), *The Developmental State*, Ithaca: Cornell University Press, 1999, 1-31.

4. Alice Amsden, Ibid., note 1.
5. Josephine Smart and Alan Smart, "Personal Relations and Divergent Economies : A Case Study of Hong Kong Investment in South China", *International Journal of Urban and Regional Research*, 15, 1991, 216-233.
6. Yimin Lin, "Economic Institutional Change in Post-Mao China", *Asian Perspective*, 25 (4), 2001, 33-66.
7. Yimin Lin, Ibid., note 6.
8. John McMillan and Barry Naughton, "How to Reform a Planned Economy : Lessons from China", *Oxford Review of Economic Policy*, 8, 1992, 781-807.
9. Andrew Walder, *China's Transitional Economy*, London : Oxford University Press, 1996, 9.
10. Kyung-Sup Chang, "The Politics of Partial Marketization : State and Class Relations in Post-Mao China", *Asian Perspective*, 25 (4), 2001, 239-268.
11. George Lin, "Regional Integration in South China", *Asian Perspective*, 25 (4), 2001, 93-126.
12. George Lin, Ibid., note 11.
13. Alvin Y. So, "China Under the Shadow of the Asian Financial Crisis : Retreat from Economic and Political Liberalism", *Asian Perspectives*, 23 (2), 1999 83-110; and *Far Eastern Economic Review*, *Asia 2002 Yearbook*, Hong Kong : Far Eastern Economic Review, 2001.
14. Suzanne Ogden, "Chinese Nationalism : The Precedence of Community and Identity over Individual Rights", *Asian Perspective*, 25 (4), 2001, 157-186.
15. Carsten Holz and Tim Zhu, "Assessment of the Current

State of China's Economic Reforms", Alvin Y. So (ed.), *China's Developmental Miracle : Origins, Transformations and Challenges,* Armonk : M. E. Sharpe, Forthcoming.

16. David S.G. Goodman, "The People's Republic of China : The Party-State, Capitalist Revolution and New Entrepreneurs", Richard Robison and David S.G. Goodman (eds.), *The New Rich in Asia,* London : Routledge, 1996, 225-242.

17. Jane Duckett, "Bureaucrats in Business, Chinese Style", *World Development,* 29, 2001, 23-37.

18. Xueliang Ding, "Systemic Irregularity and Spontaneous Property Transformation in the Chinese Financial System", *China Quarterly,* 163, 2000; and Xueliang Ding, "The Illicit Asset Stripping of Chinese State Firms", *The China Journal,* 43, 2000, 1-28.

19. Corinna-Barbara Francis, "Quasi-Public, Quasi-Private Trends in Emerging Market Economies", *Comparative Politics,* 33, 2001, 275-294.

20. David S.G. Goodman, "Centre and Periphery after Twenty Years of Reform : Redefining the Chinese Polity", Paper presented to the conference entitled "Centre-Periphery Relations in China", The Chinese University of Hong Kong, March 24-25, 2000.

21. Kam Wing Chan, "Recent Migration in China : Patterns, Trends and Policies", *Asian Perspective,* 25 (4), 2001, 127-156.

22. Kyung-Sup Chang, Ibid., note 10.

23. Suzanne Ogden, Ibid., note 14.

24. Kam Wing Chan, Ibid., note 21.

****

2

Globalization and HIV/AIDS: Implications for Development in Africa

*Ayodele Samuel Jegede**
*Adeyinka Oladayo Bankole***
*Olabisi Prisca Adejumo****

1. Introduction

The world has witnessed, in the last two decades more than ever before, great changes in the economic, political, social, cultural and ideological realms. The phenomenon popularly tagged 'Globalization' has brought about sporadic development in the communication, transportation, technology and more importantly high-level interaction of people of diverse continents and races. *Globalization* as a phenomenon describes ideas and processes that operates internationally on the political, cultural and the economic level. The term, which is closely associated with the re-emergence of liberal economic and social thought, with its emphasis on the individual and on the economic market, began about five hundred years ago with the rise of capitalism and the expansion of European colonialism that has greatly accelerated communication between countries[1]. The events of the late 20th century and emerging 21st century is only to ensure the rapid acceleration and intensification of the process of drawing countries together.

* Department of Sociology, Faculty of the Social Sciences, University of Ibaadan, Ibadan, Nigeria.

** Department of Sociology, Faculty of the Social Sciences, University of Ibaadan, Ibadan, Nigeria.

*** Department of Nursing, Faculty of Basic Medical Sciences, College of Medicine, University of Ibadan, Ibadan, Nigeria.

Globalization is a universally emerging system characterized by interdependence, flow of exchange, the role of new technologies, the integration of markets (economy), the shrinking of time and space, particularly the intensification of worldwide social relations which link distant localities in such a way that local happenings are shaped by events occurring miles away and vice versa.

No generally acceptable definition has been found for the issue of globalization. This difficulty is not only because it is a social science concept that is as usual elusive to define but because of its multidimensionality. Secondly, there is difficulty in whether to regard it as a recent concept or to see it as a concept that has been defining or describing social processes since about the 1500's[2]. Wallerstein[3] similarly share the opinion that 'globalization is a misleading concept, since what is described as globalization has been happening for 500 years.' A critical assessment of the contemporary economic history of Africa reveals that, what is today known as globalization, is neither a new notion nor a novelty[4]. From this perspective, colonialism and imperialism would constitute forms of globalization, and it should be noted that in all these systems, nations survived by their capacity for rapid adaptation to the dictates of economic and political changes. Thirdly, the implications of globalization are so phenomenal that a 'one-dimensional' definition may not capture their full import.

The concept has been defined as *tendencies to a worldwide reach impact or connectedness of social phenomena or to a world-encompassing awareness among social actors*[5]. It is also described as the *tremendous revolutionary changes that have affected our planet as a result of changes that have also taken place in information and communication technologies – processes that have, cumulatively, led to the villagization of the globe*[6]. Barnett[7] in like manner listed out four distinct definitions common in the literature:

(i) The intensification of global linkages across a wide sphere - across transnational corporate business structures, international finances, people mobility (migration, tourism), global cultural exchange, global environmental issues, and technology and electronic communication; (ii) Globalization not only refers to economic processes or the development of economic institutions, but also describes the interconnection between individual life and global features; the process of increasing economic, political, and social interdependence and global integration that takes place as capital, traded goods, persons, concepts, images, ideas and values diffuse across state boundaries. Routes of globalization are in the industrial revolution and laissez-faire economic policies of the last century; (iii) Globalization and liberalization are a fast, new express train and countries have been told that all they need to do was get on aboard...those that fail to get aboard will find themselves marginalized in the world community and world economy; (iv) Globalization is not a new phenomenon (the 16th and late 19th centuries are both characterized by the development of communication, transportation, and production systems) but the present era has distinctive features. Shrinking space, shrinking time and disappearing borders are linking people's lives more deeply, more intensely, more immediately than ever before.

To appreciate the linkage between globalization, HIV/AIDS and national development, a peep into Gidden's[8] would suffice. Giddens[9] gave a simple demonstration of what globalization is about and how it affects every individual. According to him, an individual sipping a cup of coffee is caught up in an extremely complicated set of *social and economic relationships* stretching worldwide. The production, transportation and distribution of coffee require continuous transaction between many people thousands of miles away from the coffee drinker. Similarly, the diversity of goods which people in the West and many parts of the world have come to take for granted as available for anyone with the money to buy, depends on amazingly complex economic connections stretching across the world. The products on display have been made in, or use ingredients or parts from a hundred different countries. All these are regularly transported across the globe[10]. The emphasis from the onset therefore is that many aspects of human lives are now affected by worldwide trading exchanges and communication. The emergence and spread/transmission of global diseases such as HIV/AIDS ravaging the people of the world today is no exception.

It is the position of this paper that epidemics such as HIV/AIDS and their impact do not take place in isolation. They need to be related to other events — changes in political regime, new ideas, global warming, and the global distribution of power. These events are interwoven and can no longer deal with issues piecemeal while we claim to have given them full attention. This paper therefore critically demonstrates HIV/AIDS as a global disease affecting negatively national development in many ways. Some of which is the depletion of available human resources and demanding a significant proportion of the global resources in the effort to combat it. Internationally, Barnett[11] identified fear about "AIDS refugees" who may flood the countries of the North on "therapeutic pilgrimage" in search of treatment. The problem of HIV/AIDS is occupying prominent position in global heath agenda. It has now been even classified as security issue with its transnational effect taken into consideration. The concern is not only in its infectious tendency but due to lack of appropriate cure despite scientific height. Hence, the epidemic is reducing life expectancy while increasing the burden and the number of orphan children.

HIV/AIDS is no longer an urban problem. It has now spread to rural areas and affects the severity of the rural life while disrupting their economic, social and psychological structures. Since majority of the African population are living in the rural areas, there is need to pay attention to a disease that knows no bound. In fact, "few human tragedies in recent history have focused the world's attention on HIV/AIDS. For sub-Saharan Africa, the spread of the epidemic came at a time when many of its nations are not well equipped to respond effectively. The problem becomes more important in Africa where most of its nations are especially saddled with undue responsibilities of coping with internal strife, debt burden, economic and social misfortunes, refugees and complete collapse of social amenities"[12].

It was in recognition of this fact that the Clinton Administration designated AIDS as a threat to the United States of America national security because of its catastrophic social consequences, particularly in the developing world. It was argued that "the administration fears the AIDS pandemic could grow to even more devastating proportions eventually toppling governments, ruining economies, fuelling ethnic wars and seriously undermining free-market democracies[13].

Although interactions between the epidemic and overall development have been acknowledged, the linkages to international relations have received less attention because the epidemic was perceived as being largely health. The existing evidence of spread of the epidemic is even often overlooked because of poor data, the irregular patterns of the spread and perceived lower prevalence in the rural, than in the urban areas. As a result of this new dimension of the spread of the epidemic in a continent where the main stay of the economy is agrarian, the impacts could be enormous. Generally, little is known about impacts of HIV/AIDS in Africa[14].

The paper, therefore, explores the impact of the HIV/AIDS epidemic on the entire population and highlights the consequences for development in Africa. It also examines the need for international cooperation in prevention and control of HIV/AIDS between African countries and the America nation since the U.S. herself has defined HIV/AIDS as a "threat to national security" from the point of view of the spread of the disease in developing nations. Impact in this paper means the direct consequences of HIV/AIDS on the population or its segment and resultant effect on the society. Structural functionalist perspective is adopted to discuss the data since the paper focuses on structural themes as social, economic, political, psychological and health. The effect of HIV/AIDS on any of these structures will alter the effectiveness of the others and the entire social system.

2. Materials and Methods

Secondary source of data collection was done by reviewing existing data. Selected study findings on the impacts of HIV/AIDS on the African population, families, economy, policy, and social services are reiterated and fundamental problems and major challenges for development and security are highlighted. The scope of the review was limited to impact assessment and did not include knowledge, attitude to HIV/AIDS or other aspects like care and support. For this study, both empirical study and policy papers were reviewed. Content analysis was the main method of data analysis. Hence, the impact was examined as follows: unemployment, economic impact including health budget, debt burden, reduced labour force, reduced family budget/income; political impact including shift in government policy, debt; and health impact (morbidity and mortality).

3. Findings

3.1 Social Impact

a. *Unemployment Impact:* Current situation in Africa gives room for concern about the future of PLWHA. HIV/AIDS has now become a yardstick for employment as many employers of labour are intolerant of PLWHA. For instance, a Nigerian Staff Nurse lost her job due to her HIV-seropositive status. To worsen her condition, she couldn't get redress in the law court. The situation is as bad as that in many African countries. This process has rendered many unemployed in Africa thus compounding the labour market.

b. *Educational Impact:* As teachers die and orphans drop out of school, gains in literacy and enrolment ratios are being quickly eroded. Onishi in an article in the *New York Times* examined the threat of HIV/AIDS to education in sub-Saharan Africa, data have shown that "in some of the worst affected countries nearly one half of children who lose their parents to HIV/AIDS drop out of school". The journalist visited a school in a village in Cote d'Ivoire village and found that the school had been closed down since 1997 when the last teacher died of AIDS. According to 1998 official report, six teachers were dying per week of AIDS and 10 percent of all teachers deaths were AIDS related. The children of Cote d'Ivoire are not the only ones to find their schools closed by AIDS. In 1999, 860,000 children in Sub-Saharan Africa were estimated to have lost their teachers to AIDS[15]. The worst affected countries are South Africa, Zimbabwe and Nigeria where more than 85,000 children lost their teachers. Also in Zambia during the first 10 months of 1998, 1,200 teachers died of AIDS[16]. In fact, a recent study on occupational group and HIV/AIDS prevalence in Nigeria show that the disease is affecting both students and teachers unabated[17].

3.2 Economic Impact

a. *Macro-Economic Aspect:* Advent of HIV/AIDS exerts serious pressure on the macro-economic performance of already troubled economic system of the African countries. The difficulties to mobilize the necessary resources to control the epidemic and mitigate its effects may result in economic crisis. Countries with adult prevalence rates of less than 5 percent will experience only a modest impact on the GDP growth rate because it is often said "a healthy nation is a wealthy nation". However, as prevalence rises UNAIDS estimates that a prevalence rate of 20 percent or more leads to a decline in the GDP growth rate with 2 percent a year, and in per capita income with 1 percent[18] compared to historical economic performance in sub-Saharan Africa, such losses are very significant. The World Bank and UNAIDS estimated that HIV/AIDS reduces per capita income growth in Africa by at least 0.5 percent; South Africa, the economic power house of Africa and home to nearly 5 million PLWHA will likely have its GDP lower by 17 percent in 2010 due to HIV/AIDS. South Africa will loose US $22 billion..."[19].

b. *Increased Health Budgets:* HIV/AIDS being a health problem exerts a serious strain on health budgets of African countries as enormous resources is required to meet its needs. This is apart from the loss experienced in the area of personnel which usually requires retraining. For instance, a Zambia report indicates that deaths among health workers had increased 13-fold from 1980 to 1990 mainly because of AIDS[20]. Also in South Africa, one fifth of all registered nurses in the country were HIV positive. In one nursing school half of the first year students were infected. Another report describes the staffing situation in a ward for AIDS-sick women at a Malawi hospital. According to the report, "during the past year the ward had lost 2 nurses, one laboratory technician, one electrician and two hospital attendants in AIDS". It was also reported that in a graduate class of 20, three were dead and two were ill of AIDS. In fact, a study in Nigeria shows that more than half 52.4 percent of the nurse's respondents had anxiety about caring for HIV/AIDS patients due to fear of infection[21].

To adequately care for HIV/AIDS as it is sophisticated equipments and drugs are required which cost huge amount of money. In Africa most of the anti-retroviral drugs are unaffordable. While the drugs are available in the US, they are still out of reach in Africa. Even cost of testing is enormous due to cost of testing kits. For instance, it costs an average of N1,5000 about $10 to test for HIV in Nigeria. As a result it becomes very difficult for government to provide free testing services while the citizens cannot afford its cost.

c. *Reduced Labour Force:* It has been projected that in sub-Saharan Africa, the size of the labour force will be 10 to 30 percent smaller by 2020 than it would have been without HIV/AIDS[22]. This was attributed to erosion of human capital, loss of skilled and experienced workers and reduction in productivity which are argued to result in a mismatch between human resources and labour requirements with grave consequences for the private sector and public sector employers. The problem of child labour has been argued to be exacerbated by HIV/AIDS as children who have lost their parents have to rely on themselves for basic survival[23].

d. *Increased Family Budget:* Data have shown that most of the infections and deaths resulting from AIDS affect men and women in the prime of their lives, hitherto energetic bread winners, politicians, community leaders, husbands and wives[24]. According to the World Bank and UNAIDS, by the time the rate of infection reach 20 percent in a country, prior gains in health and longevity are wiped out. Data have shown that at least 10 African countries have 20 percent of their adult citizens living with HIV/AIDS. Food supply at household level becomes increasingly difficult as both the sick and care givers fail to earn enough income to support their families[25].

It has been argued that families and communities are under increasing economic difficulties due to prolonged sickness and lack of income. Its family members become sick, economic activities get more shrink in the family. Farm holdings will deteriorate due to lack of proper care. In fact, the affected families are further affected and impoverished due to high cost of funerals, including absences from work to attend burial ceremonies. As economic opportunities are drying up, under-employed or jobless individuals are likely to adopt fatalistic attitude to life including sexual indiscretions. The cost of grandmothers, most of them living in abject poverty, catering to millions of AIDS orphans, also exert great pressure on family budget. As a result children are forced into exploitative labour market situations to earn extra income for their families. Because young female workers are particularly vulnerable to sexual abuse thus this paves way to prostitution as observed in a recent study in Nigeria[26].

e. *Food Security:* HIV/AIDS epidemic is exerting undue pressure on agriculture. It is contributing to the existing problem of malnutrition in Africa while adding to the burden of rural women especially those who head farm households. In Africa, reduced food production is already being reported in many countries affected by HIV/AIDS. But the irony of the matter is that HIV infected persons can live better with good nutrition which many people have no access to in Africa.

3.3 Political Impact

a. *Governance Issue :* HIV/AIDS has serious problem on the rapidity of government to divert basic social services. Human resources are lost, public resources reduced and budgets diverted towards coping with the impact. Also, the organizational survival of civil society institutions is under threat with a corresponding impact on democracy[27].

   Recently many African countries have diverted attention to HIV/AIDS at the expense of other essential social services. The government of Nigeria has declared full support for the prevention and control of the disease. As a result a retreat was held in Abuja recently bringing together stakeholders, local and international.

The Nigerian government is also working on a National Plan of Action (NPA) on HIV/AIDS aside from the usual national health and population policy. According to Minister of Health "we have put the required machinery in place to relentlessly fight the epidemics[28]. According to Soyinka[29] "a notable change in the attitude of the government came in 2001 when President Obasanjo showed political maturity and leadership by coming out boldly to commit himself and his government to the fight against AIDS in Nigeria and the African continent. President Obasanjo's input led to the acceptance of the rich nation's responsibilities to the poorer nations and which led to the creation of the Global Fund Against AIDS". All these attempts a shift in government policies to respond to a disease posing threat to the existence of human race.

According to Fuerth in an interview with the Post Newspaper in the US[30], "AIDS in Africa is a slow-motion destruction affecting the viability of these societies and the stability of the region. And it isn't as if this disease is going to stay put in sub-Saharan Africa. This report suggests that AIDS is a worldwide affair which may not stop its incursion into Africa but have its toll on other parts of the world. "Based on current trends, South Asia and the former Soviet Union could also be on a course to disaster with the HIV-infected population in Russia alone projected to exceed 1 million by the end of 2000. In fact, it was argued, "the thing that's most staggering, and people are just beginning to grasp, is that Africa is the tip of the iceberg". In fact, the January intelligence report posted on the CIA's web site suggest a relationship between AIDS and government stability, saying the "relationship between disease and political instability is indirect, but real". The report stated further that the consequences of AIDS appear to have "a particularly strong correlation with the likelihood of state failure in partial democracies". AIDS plague however, has a tendency for revolutionary wars, ethnic or inter-tribal wars, genocides and disruptive regime transitions if adequate precautions are not taken.

b. *Debt Burden* : The economic burden of HIV/AIDS in Africa is a serious problem for the continent. As the scourge of the disease begins to spread, it puts more burden on the budget than government can source for locally. As a result African governments have to seek external fund which adds to the existing debt burden plaguing the continent. The irony of the matter is that development aid has reduced drastically. Data have shown that "as the AIDS killing fields in Africa grew, development assistance from rich nations fell from $32 per person in 1990 to $19 now. Income per capita in Africa shrunk from $552 in 1991 to $474 in 2000. Commodity prices, the major non-oil exports of many African countries fell by 60 percent in the last two decades[31]. Furthermore, African countries face tremendous trade barrier in America and Europe from massive agricultural subsidies. In addition, "Africa also pays an estimated $13 billion a year in debt repayments, forcing countries to reduce expenditures in healthcare and education. To make matters worse, many African countries squandered their foreign exchange earnings in dubious projects and corruption"[32]. According to the report, the economic impact of HIV/AIDS is just beginning since most of the asymptomatic carriers of HIV will become ill in the next few years and this will increase health budget and the need for financial assistance from rich nations. For instance, in an attempt to forestall further spread of HIV/AIDS the Nigerian government has just received a US$90 million World Bank loan to fight the disease.

3.4 Health Impact

Health impact can be viewed from morbidity and mortality point of view. In fact, HIV/AIDS is generally referred to as "killer disease". Data has shown that more than 16 million people have died from AIDS since the 1980s of which 60 percent of them are in sub-Saharan Africa[33].

AIDS has significantly shortened the life expectancy in many countries. For example, in Namibia, the life expectancy without AIDS is 70.1 years but has reduced to 38.9 years since the inception of HIV/AIDS, 69.5 years before AIDS in Zimbabwe and 38.8 years after. The table below shows the percentages of people infected with HIV or who are suffering from AIDS in some countries.

Table : Percentage of People infected with HIV or who are suffering from AIDS in some Countries

Country	Percentage
Zimbabwe	25.9
Botswana	25.1
Namibia	19.4
Zambia	19.1
South Africa	12.9
India	0.82
United States	0.76

Source: *The Washington Post, World Bank, WHO, UNICEF, USAID*

According to world data there is a sharp contrast between the African countries and America. In fact, it has been argued that "AIDS will alter the demographic prospects of some 20-30 African countries. Among the most seriously affected are Botswana, Kenya, Malawi, Uganda, Zambia and Zimbabwe. The list is likely to become longer with time.

World population estimates and projections of the United

Nations in 1994 the population seriously affected sub-Saharan African countries was projected to be about four percent less in 2005 than it would have been without AIDS. The US Bureau of the Census International Programs Centre (CIPC) analysis has pointed to a larger impact from AIDS in some countries than previously anticipated. "If these new projections prove true, the population of sub-Saharan Africa in 2025 could well be reduced by some 100 million below what had been expected just few years ago" (IPC).

4. Discussion

In the history of mankind there is no known disease or tragedy that has ever attracted global attention as does HIV/AIDS. For sub-Saharan Africa, the spread of the HIV/AIDS epidemic emerged at a time when the region is ill-equipped to respond effectively to the offensive. In fact, the problem became important in Africa, where most of its nations are burdened with how to cope with ethnic crisis, debt burden, economic and social degradation, refugee's problem, political instability and complete collapse of social amenities.

4.1 Globalization, Poverty and Health

The implications of globalization are both positive and negative. For instance, *A Report on Human Development in South Asia 2001* focusing on the theme "Globalization and Human Development" shows that despite the promises of globalization about half a billion people in South Asia have experienced a decline in their incomes during the 1990s. By contrast, only a small minority of the educated urban population benefited from the region's economic growth[34]. The press release clearly stated "as confirmed by this report and the emerging consensus from the recently concluded Financing for Development Conference in Mexico, globalization has failed the poor, promising riches but in effect delivering very little...South Asia remains home to the largest number of poor people in the world — some 515 million people. Over 40 percent of children did not reach fifth grade in the 1990s, and over one fifth of the region's population did not have access to health care services. In addition, the region has experienced increasing cases of infectious diseases, such as tuberculosis, malaria and HIV/AIDS. The press release continued, "as a result of globalization, income inequalities have widened in South Asia. The levels of human development, though improved since the 1960s, have started to stagnate or even decline. The poor are being marginalized."

According to the information posted on the Globalization Research Centre: HIV/AIDS Initiative, HIV/AIDS is an acknowledged global problem. No race on earth can claim to have been spared. Globally, over 42 million people are living with HIV/AIDS, 29 million of whom are on the African continent. The pandemic has already claimed over 3 million lives. The magnitude of the impact of the spread of HIV/AIDS specifically represents the extent to which dealing with the pandemic is a crisis for Africa. The HIV/AIDS Initiative of the Globalization Research Center- Africa is an attempt to contribute towards investigating solutions to this problem. HIV/AIDS is a problem with multifaceted dimensions, all of which have global implications.

Although, Barnett[35] stated that there is very little appreciation of how AIDS impact is already affecting many societies now and into the future, others as represented by the view in UCLA Globalization Research Centre-Africa[36] opined that today, the magnitude of the HIV/AIDS pandemic in Africa has turned the disease into a generational threat to future well being in a number of countries. This is because as productive members of society succumb to the disease, a whole generation of children throughout the world is losing parents, extended family and other caretakers to AIDS, thereby threatening the whole fabric of society. For more than a decade, various politicians, scientists, scholars and policymakers have attempted to understand this pandemic, to develop strategies for treating the disease, to deal with the economic, social and political impacts, and to devise approaches for preventing the spread of HIV/AIDS. In both scholarly and policy circles debates rage over how to stem the pandemic. Some suggest that the most immediate need is to treat those who are presently infected, perhaps with new miracle drugs. Others are concerned with the ethics of the HIV/AIDS crisis. Still others are concerned with understanding the political economy of the disease, or with strategies for prevention of HIV/AIDS now and in the future. Despite increased international attention and financial resources addressing the widespread problem of HIV/AIDS, the full, long term, and developmental impact of the pandemic remains under examined. There is need for more research on the longer term economic and social trends created by HIV/AIDS as well as the policy implications for governments, donor agencies, civil society and academic institutions. This is particularly the case given the present trends in sub-Saharan African countries where infection rates have risen past fifteen to twenty percent among adults. Thus, the unprecedented scale of the spread of the disease, particularly in many parts of Africa, as well as the slow onset nature of its impact, has a generational impact[37].

In the State of South Africa Report[38] a comprehensive overview of the most important population challenges facing South Africa today, and their implications was presented. Particularly, the Report finds that HIV/AIDS is dynamically related to the country's ability to respond to globalization, migration, and environmental degradation. It argues however that the perceived negative impacts of globalization, international migration and HIV/AIDS on sustainable human development can be mitigated. According to the report, many of the government's current programmes hold the key to long-term sustainable development and growth for the country.

Thus, the study of African immigration enables the study of some of the antimonies of globalization within the contemporary world system. To describe African immigration as part of the antinomies of globalization is to acknowledge that there are fundamental contradictions integral to the process of globalization. On the one hand, it is clear that many scholars assume that the process has positive consequences, paradoxically, there is clear evidence of its having negative consequences on the lives of many people who live marginal lives in the impoverished countries in Africa, Asia, Latin America, the Middle East, the Caribbean, and even in Western Europe and North America. Further, the negative and positive consequences of globalization often relate, one to the other in a dialectical manner[45]. It is a fact that globalization produces wealth in some parts of the world and at the same time produces poverty in other world's region. Access and exposure to technological innovation is as much a consequence of globalization, as is the lack of access to technology. It is as much a consequence of globalization that whole areas of the third world are no more than labour reserves for the advanced industrial, more affluent countries, as it is for other areas of the world to be magnets that draw migrants and immigrants that seek an end to the problems of unemployment and underemployment.

A probe into the factor(s) precipitating Africans' immigration into US, for instance, in the second half of the 20th century demonstrates the changing magnitude of poverty situation in the former. A number of factors such as economic, social, or political motivations *push* immigrants into leaving their countries of origin and settling in a new country, while others *pull* them into seeking immigration to a given country[39]. Push factors that stimulate migration from Africa include low pay, the lack of employment, underemployment, the absence of family members due to prior migration, and exposure to endemic violence, persecution and oppression. Pull factors also include the possibility of earning a higher income, finding employment, joining family members and hope for freedom from violence, persecution and oppression. Okome[40] posits that after the Second World War and during the period of the nationalist anti-colonial struggle for independence, Africans who traveled to the U.S. can be better described as migrants who sought education, or traveled for business or leisure. These migrants returned to their home countries once their objectives had been accomplished. Today, US consulates in African countries are swamped with Africans that seek rapid and immediate exit from their respective countries. Many do not have any plans to return home, except for brief visits, if at all. Some cannot even return anytime in the near future because they lack the visas that would enable them to travel back home once they had left. There is indeed a qualitative difference between the African migration that intensified in the period after the Second World War, and today's immigration from the African continent.

Another major event in many African nations intricately connected to globalization and having implication for the prevalence of HIV/AIDS is war. Civil wars, human rights violations and repression are push factors that also causes international migration, thus facilitating the spread of the disease. During the Nigerian civil war, many from the Biafra migrated to Western countries, including the US. The Liberian civil war, the Somalian conflict, and the Eritrean-Ethiopian are other instances where increased immigration was generated as a result of war. Wars tend to create more immigration, as well as a huge refugee population, within the continent of Africa than could ever be experienced outside the continent. Furthermore, Human rights violations and repression also generate the desire to migrate, which is met sometimes by the receptivity of Western nations to certain categories of dissidents. In the heydays of apartheid, many anti-apartheid activists fled to the West. Similarly, dissidents have had to flee neocolonial, one-party, or dictatorial states of Africa. Uganda, Kenya, Ghana, and more recently, Nigeria, are sources of this kind of immigration. From 1986 to 1999, Nigeria had regimes in power that dealt with opposition by sponsoring such high levels of repression that their most uncompromising opponents were forced to take to their heels. Thus, the frequent assemblage of allied forces and frequent contact of people of different race facilitates more often than not the spread of the disease.

What globalization has meant for Africa and Africans is also that there have been drastic restrictions on the right to self-determination and to meaningful participation in making decisions on how to properly manage the world's economy *and issues directly affecting them* (our emphasis)[41]. Participating in the global economy extracts costs from majority of the citizens of African countries. This majority suffers losses in income, employment, upward mobility, health, hope, their options are significantly reduced. However, a minority gains most of the benefits of globalization by virtue of having the desired profile for success.

Barnett[42] gave two broad views of how globalization affects health. The first sees the increased interdependence attendant upon globalization resulting in an increased willingness of nations to work together in pursuit of improved health because this would serve their rational self-interest. The view offers an optimistic analysis of the health benefits of globalization to poor countries and to poor communities in rich countries. This view argues that increased pace of cross-national exchanges should facilitate diffusion of technological innovations such as new and effective contraceptive methods, techniques for enabling access to clean water, inexpensive refrigeration, efficient transport and communication technologies, and new and effective systems for prevention and treatment of infectious disease.

The second view is a contrast and a pessimistic view that sees globalization as a phenomenon, which because of the increasing loss of sovereignty by nation states means that states are less willing to pool resources. Thus, leading to less cooperation and more protectionism, increased competition and insistence in maintaining those spheres of influence that seem intact...The more ready availability of large profits from treatments of disease in rich countries and communities has meant that — for example — there has been markedly less attention to the needs of communities and countries which have lower ability to express their needs through markets. Thomas[43] argued that the pursuit of an HIV/AIDS vaccine has been of less interest to big pharmaceutical companies. These stand to profit more from development of treatments than vaccines. Hence, Third World societies especially, are confronted with a great challenge in trying to ensure access to drugs through market mechanisms. Barnett[44] submit that the fate of the Global Fund for TB, Malaria and HIV/AIDS, which was an outcome of the UNGASS meeting in 2001, still hangs in the balance as the rate of commitment from the main donor countries remains disappointing.

4.2 Implications of Globalization for Sustainable Health Care Delivery and HIV/AIDS Prevention in Africa

There is no doubting the fact that the world has become in important respects a *single social system*, as a result of growing ties of interdependence, which now affect virtually everyone. The global system is not just an *environment* within which particular societies — like Britain — develop and change. The social, political, and economic connections which cross-cut borders between countries decisively condition the fate of those living within each of them[45]. Globalization of social relations is primarily about reordering of time and distance in social life, this leading to increasing influence of human lives by events happening far away from the social contexts in which they carry out their day-to-day activities. However, the reality of the fact that the events or processes that created the Third World societies are still present with the continent today, perhaps in another guise, calls for a critical appraisal of the way out of her poverty.

More than ever before, there is the increasing agitation towards fashioning out a new course for the development of African nations – the latest of which is the New Partnership for Africa Development (NEPAD) — most of whom are at present impoverished and being ravaged by diseases. In tackling the problems, Asante-Darko[46] states that desire for a renaissance in present-day Africa must be evaluated against the background of forty years of post-independence economic delusion and political chaos. He warned that the continent's mediocre economic performance and its continued and increasing marginalization in the international economic order is likely to be intensified and consummated by the present trend towards globalization unless viable and novel alternatives are pursued. Asante-Darko[47] quoted a writer thus :

Clearly globalization poses a grave challenge to Africa's ability to achieve the progress, which the spirit of Enlightenment promises all of mankind. Over the past decade or so the continent's intellectuals have been preoccupied with the internal dynamics of the crisis. Apparently oblivious of the global context of the continent's crisis, we have pursued the World Bank's agenda and researched and debated ad infinitum issues such as Africa's external debts, corruption, authoritarianism, civil society, constitutionalism, civil wars, ethnicity, structural adjustment and democracy while the continent's crises continue to worsen, and the suffering of its people deepened[48].

Many scholars, genuine African leaders and public commentators have at various times shared this opinion. Such is represented by the opinion of Adams Oshiomole, the President of the Nigeria Labour Congress calling with regards to globalization and Africa/Nigeria's membership of the World Trade Organization (WTO) for :

The need to strategize on the challenges posed by this new phenomenon called globalization under which Africa is a net exporter of jobs and even capital through unrestrained imports and divestment. ...In another word, unemployment, collapse of industries and the attendant social unrest are our main gains from our membership of WTO.http://www.africamigration.com / m_okome_globalization_01.htm - _edn34 Poverty, diseases, conflicts, HIV/AIDS and wars have beset African countries, saddling its labor unions "with the enormous task of ensuring fairness, social justice in our respective countries often under hostile political and economic environment. Although richly endowed with human and natural resources, Ghana and Nigeria, like many other African countries, "are struggling under the weight of mass poverty caused by inequitable distribution and reckless squandering of the nation's huge resources"[49].

Economically, HIV/AIDS afflicts the most productive members of society. This has implications for national productivity. Farming has been disrupted exacerbating the food insecurity situation in Africa. Teachers and other professionals are lost, undermining the already fragile technical human resource base for Africa. HIV/AIDS undermines national budgets owing to the high costs of dealing with the consequences of the pandemic. Households are impoverished by the high cost of dealing with the health consequences of the pandemic and the limitations on productivity.

It is a fact that the Western World has failed the Less Developed Countries in their 'promises' to lead them out of poverty. For instance, "one of the most eminent external efforts to solve Africa's developmental problems was when industrialized countries pledged 0.7% each of their resources to Third World development. It is noted that the implementation was not as splendid as the pledge suggested for by 1977, while Sweden, Norway and Holland remained faithful, others such as USA had reduced it to 0.22%; Germany, 0.27%; Japan, 0.21; and Switzerland, 0.19[50]. Despite this the World Bank has had profound influence on health provision in poor countries as the largest external financer of health activities in low and middle-income countries. It has also been a major voice in national and international health policy debates and an important contributor to health policy research.

Nonetheless, the approach to sustainable health care delivery in the low income countries as canvassed by Oshiomole is a "critical look at the root causes of prevalence of wars and conflict situations occasioned by ethnic and religious crises and its resultant effect of poverty and diseases that have continued to trail the sub-region in the last decade".

5. Conclusion

The paper has critically examined the issue of HIVAIDS within the context of globalization using secondary data to analyze the impacts of the pandemic in Africa. It is noted that if appropriate actions are not taken development in Africa may be an illusion. Therefore, it is suggested that African governments should combine efforts to prevent and control of the disease so that the huge resources being expended on the disease can go to development purposes. There is also the need for the international community or the world system to help Africa to tackle the disease by providing both technical and financial support in other to reduce its threat to national and international security.

Notes and References

1. State of South Africa Population Report, *Population, Poverty and HIV/AIDS: Release of the State of South Africa's Population Report*, Republic of South Africa : A Publication of the Population and Development Information Service, Department of Social Development, 2000.
2. Nuhu O Yaqub, "Review of the 2000/2001 National Human Development Report", *The Nigerian Social Scientist*, Vol. 6, No. 1 (March), 2003, pp. 41-48.
3. Wallerstein, "Opening Remarks: Legal Constraints in the

Capitalist World Economy", M. Likosky (ed.), *Transnational Legal Proceses : Globalisation and Power Disparities*, London: Butterworths Lexis Nexis, 2002, pp. 61-64.

4. Kwaku Asante-Darko, "Globalization and African Renaissance: The Challenge of Continental Strategies", *Nordic Journal of African Studies*, Vol. 8, No. 1, 1999, pp. 40–56
5. G. Therborn, "Globalizations : Dimensions, Historical Waves, Regional Effects, Normative Governance", *International Sociology*, Vol.15, No. 2, June, 2000, pp.151-179.
6. Nuhu O Yaqub, Ibid., note 2, p. 45.
7. Tony Barnett, *HIV/AIDS and Globalization: What is the epidemic telling us about economics, morality and pragmatism?* An Internet Material, 2002.
8. Anthony Giddens, *Sociology*, (Second Edition), UK : Polity Press, 1993.
9. Anthony Giddens Ibid., note 8, p. 19.
10. Anthony Giddens Ibid., note 8, p. 527.
11. Tony Barnett, Ibid., note 7.
12. FMOH, *HIV/Syphilis Sero Prevalence and STD Syndromes Sentinel Survey among PTB and STD Patients in Nigeria*, Technical Report, 2001.
13. CNN.COM US News Report, *AIDS Pandemic declared threat to U.S. National Security*, Cable News Network, U.S. April 30, 2000.
14. Baier, E. G., *Introduction : The Impact of HIV/AIDS on rural households/communities and the need for multisectoral prevention*, Rome : Food and Agriculture Organization of the United Nations (FAO), 1997.
15. UNAIDS and WHO, *AIDS epidemics update*, Population Reports, December 2000.

16. UNAIDS and WHO, Ibid., note 15.
17. Jegede, Ajuwon, *Odaibo and Olaleye, Cultural Context of HIV Transmission among the Yoruba of Southwestern Nigeria*, 2002.
18. UNAIDS and WHO, Ibid., note 15.
19. C. Akukwe and M. Foote, *HIV/AIDS in Africa (3) : Economic Impact– Constituency for Africa*, Washington DC, 2002.
20. UNAIDS and WHO, Ibid., note 15.
21. Effa-Heap, "The attitude of nurses to HIV/AIDS patients in a Nigerian University Teaching Hospital", European Study Group on Heterosexual Transmission of HIV (1992) Comparison of female-to-male and male-to-female transmission of HIV in 563 stable couples, *British Medical Journal*, 304, 2000, pp. 809-13.
22. PDR, "On the socio-economic impact of the HIV/AIDS Epidemic", *Population and Development Review*, 27 (3), 2000, pp. 619-624.
23. PDR, Ibid., note 22.
24. C. Akukwe and M. Foote, Ibid., note 19.
25. C. Akukwe and M. Foote, Ibid., note 19.
26. Jegede, Ajuwon, Odaibo and Olaleye, Ibid. note 17
27. PDR, Ibid., note 22.
28. FMOH, Ibid. note 12.
29. F. Soyinka, *Health Care System in Nigeria: Experiences as a Teacher, Researcher and Carer*, Valedictory Lecture by The African AIDS Research Network (Nigeria Chapter), March 2002.
30. CNN.COM US News Report, Ibid. note 13.
31. C. Akukwe and M. Foote, Ibid., note 19.
32. C. Akukwe and M. Foote, Ibid., note 19.
33. UNAIDS and WHO, Ibid., note 15.

34. UNDP, *Human Development Report, Globalization with a Human Face*, New York and Oxford : Oxford University Press, 1999, p.1; United Nations Development Programme (UNDP) "More should be done to make globalization work for South Asia's poor". A Press Releases. An Internet material.
35. Tony Barnett, Ibid., note 7.
36. UCLA Globalization Research Centre–Africa, "HIV/AIDS in Africa Initiative", 2003, Internet Material.
37. UCLA Globalization Research Centre–Africa, Ibid., note 36.
38. National Population Unit of the State of South Africa's Population Report, *Population, Poverty and Vulnerability*, Department of Social Development, 2000
39. Okome Mojubaolu Olufunke, "The Antinomies of Globalization : Causes of Contemporary African Immigration to the United States of America", *Irinkerindo : A Journal of African Migration*, Vol. 1, No. 1, September, 2002,
40. Okome Mojubaolu Olufunke, "African Immigration to the United States: Dimensions of Migration, Immigration and Exile", June 1, 1999, Internet Material.
41. Okome Mojubaolu Olufunke, Ibid., note 39.
42. Tony Barnett, Ibid., note 7.
43. Patricia Thomas, *Big Shot : Passion, Politics and the Struggle for an AIDS Vaccine*, New York : Public Affairs, 2001; UCLA Globalization Research Centre-Africa, "AIDS, Development and the Next Generation in Africa", 2003, Internet Material.
44. Tony Barnett, Ibid., note 7.
45. Anthony Giddens Ibid., note 8, p. 528.
46. Kwaku Asante-Darko, Ibid., note 4. p. 42.
47. Kwaku Asante-Darko, Ibid., note 4, p. 42.

48. *AAPS Newsletter*, 1998: 2; Kwaku Asante-Darko, Ibid., note 4, p. 42.
49. Okome Mojubaolu Olufunke, Ibid., note 40.
50. Kwaku Asante-Darko, Ibid., note 4, p. 44.

****

3

Globalization and the Prospects of Multicultural Coexistence and World Peace

Janja Zitnik*

1. Introduction

In this essay I do not want to quote from any of the countless reference books or influential articles discussing the questions involved. Neither do I want to dispute various definitions of terms such as "advanced country", "human progress", "individual success" or "successful society". This time I want to take a step back and see what I am actually looking at, without the help of intermediate interpretations. In most cases, scientific explanations have helped me surmount some of my ignorance in order to see further, wider and clearer. In certain cases they have prevented me from doing just that; and this is such a case. I choose to base my views of the opportunities for a global multicultural coexistence and peace on the immediate picture of human society as I see it, not from the angle of a scholar but from the angle of just an ordinary member of that society.

This is the picture I see: the globalization of capital, science, technology, information, ideas, political and social activism and other spheres of activity has brought about several global processes in the field of culture as well: a globalization of dominant cultures and languages, an international break-

* Research Counsellor, Institute for Slovenian Emigration Studies, Scientific Research Centre of the Slovenian Academy of Sciences and Arts, Novi trg 2, P.O. Box 306, SI-1001 Ljubljana, Slovenia.

through of various hitherto secluded minor cultures and a globalization of multicultural concepts. In spite of the fact that worldwide linkages in many of these spheres were established more than a century ago, scientists obviously agree that this permanent process, which has often been misinterpreted as a unique recent phenomenon, has been held responsible for more current issues than it should have been.

Irrespective of this it is evident that there is a long way to go yet. Multiculturalism as conceived in its various theories and political strategies has not been fully attained anywhere in the world. In "destination countries", members of native minorities and new immigrants from low-income parts of the world are still too often subject to suspicion, mistrust and various forms of cultural and social discrimination. On top of a vast multitude of scornful expressions invented to exclude these people from a society, the word immigrant itself (in general use) most often obtains a pejorative meaning – an attitude, which, of course, generates defensive reactions. A very similar emotional atmosphere is straining intercultural and socio-economic conflicts on a global scale. Let me support this analogy with a few facts and observations, starting from an experience of my home country.

2. The Case of Slovenia

Slovenia has been more and more concerned with the cultural well being of its emigrants. In parallel with its own moral, financial and organizational support the country expects the destination countries of its emigrants to go along with these efforts and secure them equal rights, not only within their legislation but also within their daily human attitude and practice.

Meanwhile, Slovenia itself is clearly becoming a multiethnic country as well. In the first decade after World War Two, 3.5% of the population of Slovenia was non-Slovenes. In the 1991 census their share was 12.2 %,[1] and a considerable number of the rest refrained from declaring their nationality. The largest minorities then were the Croats, the Serbs and the Moslems, and I expect the 2002 census results to show a similar national structure. While in the fifties and the sixties the social and the educational structure of immigrants from these Yugoslav republics was similar to that of the majority population in Slovenia, the later economic recession and the subsequent wars in these countries forced numerous unskilled workers to seek employment in Slovenia.

Our country has had model minority legislation for decades. But most of these laws pertain to our autochthonous minorities and not to the much larger immigrant ones. Certain laws do attempt to secure them equal rights, but in real life two people can hardly have the same opportunities when their living conditions have been anything but equal from the very beginning. The globalization of multicultural concepts has certainly had its effect on Slovenia. The number of government bodies and civil organizations whose projects tend to remedy the above mentioned situation has increased lately, which at least shows some good intentions on the part of the majority nation. Yet the actual reality at the present moment is less optimistic. The immigrants who came to Slovenia in the seventies or later, still predominantly live in lower-standard neighborhoods, they manage to obtain only lower qualification, and (due to the increasing unemployment) are lucky if they can get underpaid jobs. They mostly live second-rate lives, slightly better than those of most people in their native land from which they fled.

The xenophobia, open or concealed, is making it worse for them. In Slovenia, there are still immigrant jobs, mixed jobs and the non-immigrant ones. When immigrants apply for the latter, they are often met with reserve and distrust – as if we wanted them to stay "where they belong". The worst thing that can happen to a Slovene in this respect is to face an immigrant colleague's promotion sooner than his or her own — or, to see a young man from a close-by immigrant neighborhood, a boy fresh from high school, driving a new Mercedes - something which most people in Slovenia cannot afford. Of course the immigrants feel the same way about Slovenes, and neither they nor the Slovenes realize that isolated cases of rapid individual progress most often have nothing to do with someone's nationality.

It is always "we" and "they". We do not know our immigrants because we do not want to know them. We do not want to live in their neighborhoods, we do not ask about their problems, we do not attend their public meetings, and we do not read their poems. We do not particularly like their clothing or hairstyle and we want to look as different from them as we can. We do not appreciate their habits of life. We feel uneasy when we enter a public place where their languages prevail, and we tend to be a bit more cautious when their children make friends with our children. In certain countries or cities (eg. Germany and the traditionally multiethnic Vienna), these kinds of emotional obstructions are being fairly successfully dealt with, whereas Slovenia — in spite of its several experimental multicultural school programs to that effect - seems to have got stuck after a few initial steps. Our immigrants are our fellow-citizens, people living in our town, working in our company. Their culture is part of our country's heterogeneous culture - and this frightens us. When we are buying an apartment, we check the names on the mailboxes to see how many immigrants live in the building. When we are choosing the "right" school for our child, we check the names of other pupils to see how many immigrant children attend that school. We still avoid socializing with them; their children are still called names. They do not only grow up in social insecurity, but also in fear, in guilt, in a total lack of self-confidence. They respond with delinquency and crime, and when they don't, they are the most convenient scapegoats.

Soon after World War II when immigrants in Slovenia formed the same social class as the majority of Slovenes, there were hardly any signs of xenophobia to be observed in the country compared to the present atmosphere. Most people nowadays may not come out in the open with their negative feelings but the immigrants can still sense the effects of our concealed aversion any time anywhere. They feel that they are welcome to do their jobs properly, but not to speak about their scrapes and needs. They know that if they did speak up, they would be fired just as easily as any other manual worker in a crude capitalist system.

We feel safest with those immigrants who are not too much wealthier or too worse off than most of us. The few immigrants from countries wealthier than Slovenia, mostly qualified experts, are generally met with approval and respect because they are few and they neither "take away our jobs" or, as we often say, "enslave our workers in their foreign corporations" which are being increasingly spread all over our country. We do not resent their ways and habits, as their cultures are not too different from our own culture. (And when they are, we find them exotically attractive because they are not numerous enough to make us feel jeopardized either in the economic or in the cultural aspect.) But if some time in the future we happen to sell out most of our national economic and cultural property to them, we will begin to resent them as well although we should in fact rather attribute the lack of our economic and cultural sovereignty to the mere convenience of our easy political decisions.

In the face of our will to join the European Union, it may happen in time something similar with our national culture as what is just going on, according to an observation by Valerie Steel,[2] in the world of fashion. Ms. Steel expects the future fashion trends to become, under the influence of globalization, more and more multicultural, meaning that they will tend to combine the clothing traditions from those cultures, which until now have not been introduced into vogue. Obviously we are facing a transition of ethnic clothing characteristics from one level to another, from the level of a thousand years old regional tradition to the level of an artificial creation designed for a universal user. The point of a regional or a national garb is a regional or an ethnic identification, whereas the point of a multicultural fashion design is an identification with an exotic vogue taste which may or may not additionally indicate a specific political statement. Is it possible that our national art, literature, culture and folklore are facing a similar long-term transformation from one level to an essentially different one? Is globalization turning the essence of the ethnic into its opposite? Advocates of postmodernist interpretations of globalization seem to think so. But witnessing numerous proofs that the threat of a cultural homogenization which globalization has imposed on minor and medium-size ethnic cultures has generated an evident revitalization of those cultures, I believe that too much pessimism in this respect would be far-fetched. As we have so often heard in these past few years, it is entirely up to us.

Anyway, in the meantime we want to live well, even if with a little help from our powerful friends, and besides that — we want to feel self-confident and "on our own". And this is creating an inner conflict, which seems to have ended up in a blind alley. In fact, this conflict represents the essential need of the contemporary reality, the need of a balance between the national and the global. Of course it will take continuing efforts to establish a more or less permanent balance. But then again, while fighting our own minority battles for an equal position within the EU, perhaps we will develop a more sensitive ear for the needs of the immigrant minorities in our own country as well.

3. Co-cultural Reciprocity in a Brief Historical and Future Perspective

Tolerance Is Not Enough is the title of a famous speech presented on a cross-American lecture tour soon after World

War II by Louis Adamic (1898–1951), the most recognized Slovene emigrant writer as yet.[3] Seven years earlier he proclaimed that the United States should finally accomplish the ancient principle of 'Unity in Diversity', on the American continent probably first printed as a motto in the U.S. Foreign Language Information Service monthly called *Interpreter* (1923–1930). In its successor, the quarterly *Common Ground* (1940–1942), which was "the first American literary periodical to be devoted entirely to ethnic and intercultural matters,"[4] its editor Louis Adamic, together with his renowned team, largely advocated this principle. The quarterly brought articles in which their authors were suggesting possible ways for over sixty different nationalities living together on the common American ground to attain harmonious cultural coexistence; or in Adamic's words, "...that we sink our tap roots deep into its (i.e. America's) rich and varied cultural past and attain national stability in place of emotional hysteria..." [5] The core of the *Common Ground*'s message was that everyone should not only be allowed but also encouraged to be proud of what they are – racially and ethnically, religiously and culturally. Moreover, to compose a successful and contented heterogeneous society each member should not only accept and respect its cultural diversity but also gain from it.

As old as the idea was at that time, it was still premature for the majority of the US population. It took another thirty years before a *hunky* could proudly proclaim his or her ethnic roots without being further stigmatized by members of the Anglo-Saxon majority or a fellow immigrant minority. Nowadays, countless ethnic, religious and other specifically defined groups are still experiencing various forms of social rejection. Hundreds of books and thousands of articles have been written on xenophobia, on ethnic, religious and cultural discrimination as well as on multiculturalism and integration. As a result, it has long been recognized that the fear of the alien is a projection of self-alienation. Xenophobia has been defined as a fear of the foreign, the unfamiliar, the unknown, including that 'unknown' which has long been part of our lives and, unconsciously, of us ourselves. Once we get to know our unknown constituent elements, once the *foreign* is no longer foreign but becomes *ours* even at the conscious level, the fear disappears too. And if we were to see in modern intercultural processes an enrichment of our national culture rather than its 'pollution by foreign cultures', our mistrust and defensive aggressiveness will also disappear. The problem with this simple fact is that if people actually accepted it, they would no longer be liable to the most frequently applied strategies of mass manipulation.

If Slovenia or any other country wanted to do away with xenophobia and its symptoms, reflected in ethnic, religious and cultural discrimination of its (immigrant or native) minorities, the majority should develop more interest in getting to know the less familiar parts of the country's population. The dominant nation should learn not only about the minorities' cultural wealth but also about their existential problems. For this reason a modern multiethnic country should — while also ensuring equal opportunities of survival for ethnic cultural media — ensure a greater language transfer between the cultures which make up its heterogeneous multiethnic culture, since only in this way will it truly be possible to talk about not just a multitude of individual authentic, yet more or less isolated cultures existing within the same national boarders, but also about a well-functioning network of actual *co-cultures*, a network which would ensure the entire national population an equal access to each part of their culture. I would label this kind of cultural reciprocity within a multiethnic society as *'co-culturalism'*, rather than multiculturalism - as the latter is too often understood as a mosaic of separate particles forming a more or less abstract picture.

What would this mean in practice? Stimulating and

supporting immigrant cultures is undoubtedly positive, since it enables the development of these cultures even outside the borders of their parent countries. In order for these ethnic cultures to take an equal part in creating the complex multiethnic culture of their new homeland, they must be equally accessible to all its potential users. For this reason multiethnic countries must also give more support to the translation of literary works and various other texts by immigrants into their majority language, and to their publication in mainstream cultural media. Only in this way can the members of multiethnic societies really get to know the people with whom they actually live, with whom they share their common home, and learn what creative impulses, pressures and motivations go to make up their already tightly interwoven common culture, in which, however, there are still far too many unnecessary mental, emotional, political and administrative barriers and obstructions. A critical stand toward any element of a culture cannot be taken unless it is based on an adequate perception of the subject. Without language transparency, there can be no full perception of a culture. Furthermore, the language differentiation is still a frequent motive for stigmatization and disrespect. When we become familiar with the contents, which individual languages can and wish to express, we will be capable of an equal respect for all of them as well.

This sounds like a very old idea, a starting-point of practically every multicultural theory. The question is whether it works sufficiently well, and if not, why so.

4. Some Minor Traps of Multiculturalism (at First Hand)

Once again I am going to try and see whether some of the answers to the above question can be found within the 'multicultural experience' of my nation, this time of Slovene emigrants. The Slovene-Canadian writer, editor and cultural worker Cvetka Kocjanèiè has analyzed the experience of Slovene immigrants within the framework of Canada's multicultural policy in a series of published articles and unpublished reflections. In general terms she considers that the policy of multiculturalism in Canada has contributed enormously to making the integration of immigrants into the new environment and Canadian society as healthy as possible, reduced the effects of culture shock and the resulting mental illness among immigrants, promoted the unity of all Canadians under the slogan 'Unity in Diversity' and helped form a specifically Canadian culture which differs considerably from American culture. To immigrants of 'visible minorities' the introduction of the multiculturalism policy has opened the doors to various walks of life, which were previously closed to them — politics, the public media, the police, the army etc. The state has promoted a great many activities by immigrants and ethnic groups in a variety of ways, from guaranteeing a minimum income during the initial six-month English course, providing financial support for supplementary teaching in the mother language and the right to choose the mother tongue as an optional subject at secondary school (in the case of ethnic communities prevalent in a given area), to specially earmarked budgetary funds for other immigrant activities including the ethnic press, research, cataloguing immigrant archives, ethnic radio, the building of society premises and homes for the aged, and multicultural events (e.g. the Toronto Caravan, Folklorama in Winnipeg, Open House in St Catherines etc.).[6]

Kocjanèiè does however point out a number of shortcomings:

'Immigrant communities bring their own characteristic internal ideological frictions to multicultural institutions and thus obstruct many projects. Funds are limited and ethnic communities or individuals get them on the basis of an invitation for bids, about which immigrants are not sufficiently well informed. The amount of funds earmarked for such projects is falling from year to year. Furthermore the key for approval of requests is not sufficiently well defined – experts make the decision from individual spheres (peers: writers for writers, painters for painters, folklorists for folklore). There is a danger here that these experts may decide to give support on the basis of their own taste rather than on the basis of the interest and needs of the ethnic community. The commission is often more favorably inclined towards those who have already been active in Canadian circles (i.e. to the second generation) than to the first generation of immigrants. In theory a writer could receive financial support for a literary work in his own ethnic language, and in this case a commission of experts from his ethnic area would decide on the choice of candidate. For the relatively small Slovene community, which has had few experts in these circles, the possibility for forming expert ethnic commissions has been small. The Canadian state has for the most part treated the publishing of ethnic newspapers as something, which should be financed by subscriptions and advertisements. A similar situation has applied to radio media: ethnic radio broadcasts have not obtained direct state financial support and have maintained themselves through advertisements and funds contributed by the ethnic community. Even participation at multicultural events has proved ineffective among Slovenes since there have been too few volunteers for the demanding preparations of the one-week festivals, while state support is only received by the central organizer, who also receives the gate money from the event. Additionally ethnic festivals are dominated by 'lowbrow culture' – popular folk music, folklore, cooking, souvenirs and some token traditional crafts. Some societies have abused state support because there has not been sufficient supervision of their activities. The consequence of this is that conditions for obtaining the status of charitable organization have become tougher.

Immigrants have often claimed discrimination when for example they have failed to get the job they want. For this reason some state services are now required to employ a certain number of immigrants from visible minorities (Afro-Americans, Muslims, Native Americans etc.). The result of this is that in some places immigrants get jobs even though they are less well qualified than other Canadians. State services employ people with, for example, an imperfect command of English, while there are police officers and firemen who are not physically capable of doing their job. Under the guise of multiculturalism immigrants have demanded more and more from the state, for example the right to wear turbans in the Canadian army, the right for the children of a specific ethnic community to carry knives to school as a religious symbol, etc., and this has begun to bother other Canadians considerably. Another case of reverse discrimination is the new ghettoization of the Chinese inhabitants of Markham, a suburb of Toronto, where access to Canadian shops and offices is practically closed to non-Chinese. Business is done almost exclusively in Chinese and non-Chinese are ignored. When a local politician opposed this, they described their attitude as a reaction to the discrimination practised against them.

Under the conservative government, which coincided with a major recession in Canada, immigrants were deprived of numerous programs. For some time now Canada has been without an independent minister for immigrants; instead they come under the Ministry of Citizenship and Culture.'[7]

In Europe Sweden is undoubtedly the country, which Europeans most frequently connect with a more consistent concept of multiculturalism. The Slovene sociologist Marina Lukšiè-Hacin has published numerous articles and monographs on the Slovene immigrant experience within the framework of Swedish multiculturalism.[8] In her comparison of Swedish multiculturalism with Australian and Canadian multiculturalism she highlights some of the most obvious differences:

1. Australia and Canada have been traditional countries of immigration since the period of modern colonialism. The immigrants have come from various environments, while indigenous populations already lived in these countries. Thus an ethnically heterogeneous population has appeared.
2. Australia and Canada grew up on the foundations of modern colonialism and were subject to the conditions already described in the introduction: ethnocide and genocide directed against the indigenous population, classification of cultures using a hierarchical model with the dominant WASP (White Anglo-Saxon Protestant) culture based on the monocultural principle or Eurocentrism at the very top and proclaimed as the most developed. All of this is linked to powerful racism, stigmatization and the stigmatized identity reproduced by the dominant hegemony. The influence of attitudes and value systems from the past is still felt today. This is where Sweden has its advantages, since it does not have a direct colonial experience and is not burdened by cultural imperialism.
3. Sweden has a specific democratic system based on strong state intervention. This is the basis of the social state in which is reflected the value system of Swedish culture/society. Thus, multiculturalism in Sweden is not the result of the struggle of indigenous minorities for political and cultural rights; it is the result of the Swedish way of life and of the value system of the Swedes. The initiative in the case of Canada and Australia is on the part of the oppressed and disenfranchised; in Sweden it is more on the part of Swedish culture/society and the Swedish state.
4. The fourth difference is indirectly connected to the demands of a radical multiculturalism, which advocates egalitarian attitudes and a social society. Because of these demands it is accused of being utopian. The cultural/social

> situation in Sweden was in some ways similar to the ideal even before the introduction of a multicultural approach.
>
> Swedish multiculturalism comes into conflict with cultural relativism where the values of the minority culture come into conflict with the normative regulation of Swedish democracy. This is the tolerance threshold of Swedish multiculturalism, which to a large extent is a reflection of the system of values of Swedish culture and its attitude to violence against individuals.[9]

An example of such a conflict might be those forms of violence against women and children, which are more present in some cultures than in others. In the understanding of one minority culture the forms of violence against women and children which are perhaps prevalent in the majority culture but which in its legislation are not treated as abuses and are not counted as criminal offences (e.g. neglecting the mental needs of children and the loosening of family ties because the parents are overworked, which manifests itself in various types of compulsive behavior by parents and children such as dependency on psychoactive substances and other dependencies; social and emotional immaturity of parents and a high divorce rate, which is reflected in the mental traumas suffered by children, for which no-one is criminally liable; an imbalance between the responsibility of parents in the face of the changed position of working mothers in the family, to whom involuntary overburdening can cause mental and physical damage) are more unacceptable than those which are perhaps more present in their own minority culture (e.g. physical violence). The decision on which forms of violence or abuse are unacceptable still lies in the end with the majority culture, with its 'own' legislation. The changing of cultures through mutual contact is a gradual and usually relatively lengthy process.

The experience of Slovene immigrants in Sweden also has its darker sides. Avguština Budja, writer and a leading figure in Slovene cultural circles in the Swedish town of Landskrona, writes:

'Swedish immigration reforms have mostly been aimed at three particular political goals, which were defined and adopted in 1975: *equality, freedom to choose, and co-operation*. These goals apply to the entire population of Sweden, regardless of ethnic origin and background. But goals are one thing and reality another. Swedish immigration policy has been based on the assumption that people who have settled there for any of a number of reasons and have received a residential permit will also stay there. Gunnar Alsmark, one of the leading ethnologists in Sweden comments: Swedish society does not wish to throw immigrants out of the country, on the contrary, it wishes to throw them into the country and make them Swedish by force. At the same time, the state preaches equality, freedom to choose, and co-operation to the entire population. The very attitude of the Swedish towards immigrants has been full of contradictions and conflicts from the very beginning. The way in which Swedish society takes care of its immigrants is oppressive rather than democratic,[10] and, as Alsmark and many other experts maintain, the freedom to choose is therefore nearer to assimilation than integration.

It can be said that in Sweden in recent years knowledge of Swedish has become an indicator of social class, which in most cases is detrimental for immigrants. It is absurd that the majority of foreigners who have arrived in Sweden in the last decade and have enjoyed the advantage of formal (school-organized) Swedish language tuition have mastered the language better than those who have been living in Sweden for almost half a century but to whom Swedish society has not given the opportunity of learning the language in a formal environment. The latter are mostly refugees who arrived after the Second World War, and workers from the 1960s and 1970s. They helped to build up the prosperity of Swedish society together with the rest of the Swedish population, but today their value is measured mostly according to their knowledge of Swedish.

As far as the knowledge and development of the Slovene language among Slovenes in Sweden is concerned, it can be established that contact with the original country was very limited due to the geographic distance and the relatively small number of Slovenes living in Sweden. Teachers who were employed by the Swedish school authorities regardless of their actual qualifications and pedagogical abilities mostly gave extra-curricular Slovene language classes. The reason for this was of course the Swedish immigration policy, which tried to prevent Slovene immigrants and their children from returning home. In the majority of other Western European countries, Slovene teaching personnel were supplied by Slovenia itself, a fact which was also of great ideological significance.[11]

When an alternative opinion was needed in the public discussion on immigrants, only a few of them spoke Swedish sufficiently well to express their views. Furthermore, since the immigrants' command of their own language has weakened, conditions for literary creativity either in their language or in Swedish have been extremely poor. The consequence of this has been the extremely small number of (mostly rather insignificant) literary works among Slovene immigrants in Sweden.

Equally, the participation of immigrants in political activities has been far from adequate. Though it is true that the right to vote at municipal and regional elections is given to immigrants after only five years of permanent residence in Sweden, this right is only seldom exercised. This is probably caused by the lack of political candidates interested in changing the negative trends among immigrants or who themselves have an immigrant background. At the last elections, in 1994 [this was written only two years later], the percentage of immigrants among politicians was 1.5%, which contrasts sharply with the overall proportion of immigrants in the Swedish population (approximately 25%).[12]

I believe both of the above testimonies clearly indicate some of the existing obstacles which the designers of multicultural or integration policies ought to consider. On the other hand we must bear in mind that Slovene emigrants in Canada or Sweden do not represent – socially – the most or the least handicapped stratum of society in either of the two countries. Hence, their 'multicultural experience' has by no means been representative of those ethnic groups, which have been exposed to the worst forms of xenophobia and discrimination.

5. The Major Trap: Economic Basis of Cultural Equality and World Peace

It is self-evident that a culture with a weak economic basis does not have the same prospects as a culture with a firm economic basis. Furthermore, cultural equality is not in the interest of those who want to preserve or increase the existing degree of social differences. The question of xenophobia, the resulting discriminations and the undesired reactions to these seems to be closely related to the question of the socio-economic order and stratification of a society. When an immigrant or a native minority presents a specific social stratum, the extreme upper or the extreme lower one, the majority finds a way of putting the blame for their disappointments with their own social system on the nationality or religious structure of those social strata, which stand out most from the average. An analogy with the psychological background of the world tensions is obvious. The feelings of national, religious, social and cultural insecurity have always been liable to demagogical abuse. The most frequent strategy of preserving conditions for political power or financial prosperity at the cost of others, be it of those in one's home country or on the other side of the globe, has been the policy of turning their attention away from the fact that they have been taken advantage of. The easiest way to keep them busy with other problems is to stir their national and religious feelings. In individual multiethnic countries political parties have been using these effective tools to consolidate their own political power on a national scale, just as the world superpowers' foreign policy has been using the same methods to consolidate their global influence in order to protect the capital they represent. Can the issues of multiculturalism and global peace culture be discussed separately from the issues of socio-economic abuse, national or international?

A multicultural coexistence and world peace are not in the interest of those 6 percent of the world population who - under the protection of their own legislation - have taken possession of 59 percent of the world material goods. If the world wants to start making its own decisions, it should probably crack this nut to begin with. This simple statistics points to the worst form of discrimination that has ever taken place anywhere. Three richest individuals possess a wealth, which is greater than the sum of the GDP (gross domestic product) of 48 poorest countries together.[13] To compare the GDP per inhabitant of five richest and five poorest countries in the world, the difference between them tripled in four decades (1950–1992). The income of the richest 20 percent of the world population was multiplied by 2.5 between 1960 and 1998, whereas the income of the poorest 20percent has remained unchanged. The number of those who can spend less than a dollar a day (1.2 billion people) has not changed in the last decade either — not to mention the share of those who have nothing at all. The number of the most discriminated people, those with less than a dollar a day, has jumped in East Europe and Middle Asia from 1 million in 1987 to 24 million in 1998. Their share in Central and South Africa and in South Asia has been slightly below half of these countries' entire population. In countries like Burkina Faso, their share is more than 60 percent.[14] When economists become cynical enough to develop one of the neo-liberal shareholder value theories which argues that if there is more bread on the table, there will be more crumbs on the floor to keep the vermin happy (which, sadly, has proved false as well), it means that we are facing not only economic cannibalism but also an ultimate and unprecedented decadence of human values on a largest scale. History has verified that whenever decadence reaches a critical point, radical changes take place.

I am convinced that it would be immoral to believe that – regardless of what kind of work I would do – my working hour could possibly be worth ten or thirty times more than another person's working hour. Any work that needs to be done but I cannot or will not do it myself, any work, which is properly done, deserves to be paid equally as my own work when it is well done. I think that the aspect of the shareholder value theory in which the only relevant feature of work is its immediate effect on the shareholder value, is unethical. I believe that greed is the core of all national and world conflicts. A new concept of human equality and democracy must be developed. Instead of protecting the interests of the few, the legislation and the diplomacy must represent general interests.

A culture of dialogue is essential. But perhaps we may all agree that a dialogue can hardly be started unless the parties involved are equal. And since most people are not equal, they can probably be expected to support aggression on their behalf for as long as they are kept, with their hands tied, in a place where no one can hear them. Furthermore, whenever there is a tyrant in the family who is willing to grant the rest of his family nothing but crumbs, he/she is not interested in dialogue either. It is up to the rest of the family to find an optimum way of replacing his/her tyrannical rules with their own democratic rules. But in order to be able to create their new rules, they have to find a consensus on some of the essential questions first. And this is where the world is being too slow at the moment.

As I see it, a global multicultural coexistence and peace can never be achieved unless they are based on a just socio-economic world order. If we want to choose peaceful dialogue and co-cultural symbiosis instead of war, terrorism and crime, the underprivileged must be set free in the first place – not by means of aggressive interventions but by means of a new perception of our common goal and of a peaceful way that can lead us there. Public opinion represents one of the two world's greatest powers. The Internet offers an opportunity for public opinion to be expressed and registered in the widest platform that has ever existed – at least potentially – out of control of those who stand on the opposite side of mankind. The problem is that only 0.2 percent of the Internet users are those from the poorest 20 percent of the world population, whereas 93.3 percent of the Internet users are those from the richest 20 percent of all people.[15] This means that the world is still having a very hard time trying to speak up. And if anyone should help it in its utmost endeavors to be heard, I believe it should be the people working in social and human sciences. I do believe it should be us.

Notes and References

1. Vesna Èopiè & Gregor Tomc, *Nacionalno poroèilo o kulturni politiki Slovenije*, Ljubljana: Ministrstvo za kulturo Republike Slovenije, 1996, p. 88.
2. Valerie Steel made this observation as a guest in a Canadian documentary serial titled *Ecce Homo*.
3. Louis Adamic, "Tolerance Is Not Enough", *T & T: Trends & Tides*, Vol. 3, January–March, 1947, pp. 14–15.
4. John L. Modic, "Louis Adamic and the Story of Common Ground", *Louis Adamiè – Symposium*, ed. Janez Stanonik, Ljubljana: Univerza Edvarda Kardelja, 1981, p. 241.
5. From Louis Adamic's editorial in the first issue of *Common Ground*, 1940.
6. Letter from Cvetka Kocjanèiè to Janja •itnik, undated

(received 24 September 2001). (Author's private archive)

7. Ibid.

8. E.g. Marina Lukšiè Hacin, *Ko tujina postane dom*, Ljubljana: Znanstveno in publicistièno središèe, 1995; Marina Lukšiè Hacin, *Zgodbe in prièevanja: Slovenci na Švedskem*, Ljubljana: Zalo•ba ZRC, 2001.

9. Marina Lukšiè Hacin, *Multikulturalizem in migracije*, Ljubljana: Zalo•ba ZRC, 1999, pp. 233–236.

10. From an article in the Swedish daily *Sydsvenska Dagbladet*, 6/1–96, p. 4.

11. In her further discussion the author states that extracurricular Slovene classes were relatively well organized between 1977 and 1991, but today they have practically gone from Swedish schools. Classes are mostly conducted only in various Slovene societies. With the reforms of 1991/92 Sweden has almost destroyed the chances of young Slovenes to grow up with the language of their ancestors with the help of an organized system (Budja, 1996: 238).

12. Avgustina Budja, "Slovenci na Svedskem", *Dve domovini / Two Homelands : Migration Studies* (Ljubljana), No. 7, 1996, pp. 221- 224.

13. Jean-Louis Laville, "Humano gospodarstvo jutrijšnjega dne", *The Unesco Courier*, Slovene edition, Vol. XXXI., No. 68, Dec. 2001, p. 13.

14. The statistics are taken from: "Neenaki zaslu•ki", *The Unesco Courier*, Slovene edition, Vol. XXXI., No. 68, Dec. 2001, pp. 14–15.

15. Ibid.

****

4

Oriental Religion in the Secular West: Globalization, New Age, and the Reenchantment of the World

*Stef Auper and Dick Houtman**

1. Introduction

Globalization changes the cultural landscape of our planet in many ways. Barber[1], for instance, argues that the globalization of western culture gives rise to all sorts of religious and political fundamentalist movements in non-western societies, producing the twins of *Jihad and McWorld* as characterizing today's world. In a similar vein, Huntington[2] speculates about a *Clash of Civilizations*, with secular and democratic western cultures increasingly conflicting with traditionally religious non-western ones. Although there is, of course, no denying that the globalization of western lifestyles and aspirations deeply affects non-western societies, one-way traffic is definitely not all there is. Non-western societies are not simply passively adapting or actively reacting to a global expansion of western culture, but are affecting western societies in many diverse ways, too.

This is especially visible in the religious domain, with late-modern western societies characterized by a remarkable interest in oriental religious ideas and practices. Extremely popular yoga is not much more than the tip of the iceberg of a 'seemingly insatiable market for things "eastern" which has emerged with

* Department of Sociology, Faculty of Social Sciences, Erasmus University, P.O. Box 1738, 3000 DR Rotterdam, the Netherlands.

a special force in the 1990s'[3]. In this paper, we discuss this current western interest in oriental religion in the allegedly disenchanted and secularized western world, primarily focusing on the New Age movement in the Netherlands. We discuss how and why those oriental religious ideas and practices have ended up in the West in the first place and how their remarkable contemporary popularity can be understood from a cultural sociological point of view[4].

2. The Western Turn to the East

2.1. Western Esotericist Perennialism

The so-called 'esoterical tradition'[5] has manifested itself in western culture since the Renaissance. According to Hanegraaff[6] this tradition of thought - that runs through movements like romanticism, occultism and theosophy — can best be understood as an undercurrent in western culture and a forerunner of the contemporary New Age movement. It has always been an epistemological alternative to 'faith' (Christianity) and 'reason' (science). In contrast with these two competing epistemological views, the esoterical tradition seeks for 'gnosis' or 'divine knowledge': 'According to this [gnosis], truth can only be found by personal, inner revelation, insight or "enlightenment". Truth can only be personally experienced: in contrast with the knowledge of reason or faith, it is in principle not generally accessible. This "inner knowing" cannot be transmitted by discursive language (this would reduce it to rational knowledge). Nor can it be the subject of faith (...) because there is in the last resort no other authority than personal, inner experience'[7]. As distinct from reason and faith, gnosis does then not assume one universally binding truth, derived from a 'reality out there' - neither truth as pre-given divine revelation ('faith'), nor truth as grasped by means of reason.

Western esotericism promotes the exploration of various religious traditions in search of their common spiritual essence or kernel. This view can be traced back to the esoterical doctrine of 'perennialism' ('philosophia perennis' or 'perennial philosophy')[8]. According to this doctrine, all religious traditions are equally valid, because they all essentially worship the same divine source. 'Spiritual truth' is thus held to transcend its various historical manifestations in established religious traditions. Hence, esotericism, in contrast with most world religions, is 'profoundly inclusivistic'[9] : its 'perennialism' puts a premium on exploring non-western religious ideas and practices. Unbound by a well-defined doctrine and motivated by perennialism, 19th-century western esotericists opened up the doors to religious diffusion and eclecticism on a global scale.

Helena Petrowna Blavatsky (1831-1891) was one of the key figures in the esoteric turn to the east at the end of the 19th century. Arguing that 'each religion is a ray of truth from the central Sun,' her New Theosophy is typically part of the esoterical tradition[10]. During her travels through India in 1868 she made contact with various Buddhists and Hindus. Those contacts and the study of oriental literature led her to conclude that 'the ultimate source of primordial wisdom is India'[11]. Whereas her earlier work, *Isis Unveiled*, is still largely inspired by ancient Egypt, in her later work, especially *The Secret Doctrine*, she strove for a synthesis between east and west. At the same time, the so-called 'American Transcendentalists' became fascinated by oriental religion, especially Hinduism and selectively incorporated concepts like karma and reincarnation into an esoteric framework. Like Blavatsky, they adopted oriental religion to a western point of view (Hanegraaff[12], Wichmann[13]). In the words of Ralph Waldo Emerson (1803-1882), probably the most famous spokesman for the 'American Transcendentalists' : 'We read the Orientals, but remain Occidental'[14].

The end of the 19th century, in short, was a crucial period for the import of oriental religion to the west. Through the work of Blavatsky, her New Theosophy and the 'American

Transcendentalists', various oriental religions got integrated in western esoterical thought.

2.2. New Age from Counter Culture to Nuclear Culture

The 1960s were a second decisive period in the popularization of oriental religion in the west. The emergence of the so-called 'counter culture' not only changed the political landscape of western societies, but had important religious ramifications as well. Whereas 'Anarchists' and 'Activists' were prominently involved in the construction and defence of new modes of social life to transcend technocratic and capitalist consumer society, 'Gnostics' represented the spiritual dimension of the counter culture[15]. 'Beat poets' such as Kerouac, Watts, and Ginsberg mixed esoterical and oriental religious ideas and introduced Buddhism to a larger audience (Puttick[16], Roszak[17]). Rejecting the traditional western types of religiosity, constructed around the Christian conception of a transcendental personal God, those Gnostics searched for meaning within the deeper layers of the self. This counter-cultural quest for spirituality, that emerged alongside its social and political dimensions, constitutes the beginning of the New Age Movement and paved the way for today's popularity of oriental practices such as yoga, Transcendental Meditation, and Tantra in late-modern western societies.

In the 1960s and 1970s New Agers still typically worked and lived in utopian communities, sheltered from the vices of technocratic and capitalist consumer society. Since the 1980s, however, this self-chosen isolation has remarkably disappeared and replaced by a religious market on which New Age centers cater for their clients' spiritual needs (Moerland[18] and Van Otterloo[19]). In 1990 there were about 200 of those centers in the Netherlands, while five years later there were already 300[20]. Not only are those centers extremely popular in contemporary western societies, but Sutcliffe and Bowman[21] even argue that in a more general sense 'contrary to predictions that New Age would go mainstream, now it's as if the mainstream is going New Age'. And judging from the remarkably increased popularity of New Age trainings in business life, this doesn't even seem a gross exaggeration (e.g., Heelas[22], Puttick[23]).

Rather than offering an escape from late-modern consumer society, today's New Age circuit is remarkably well integrated into it[24]. Books, magazines, videotapes, CD's, and health products are marketed and a wide range of courses, trainings, and therapies is on offer, aimed at improving mental and physical well being. Like postmodern hunters and gatherers, New Age consumers sample their highly varied and fleeting spiritual diets from those New Age centers. Sociologists of religion even refer to this phenomenon in terms borrowed from economics. They speak of a 'religious market'[25], a 'spiritual market'[26], 'para-cultural supply'[27], ' New Age capitalism'[28], and 'client and audience cults'[29].

2.3. Unpacking the Shelves of the Spiritual Supermarket

One of us has studied the course programs of twenty-four Dutch New Age centers a few years ago to find out what types of courses and therapies are on offer[30]. Most of the centers prove to offer a wide range of courses and trainings, while only a few specialize in a singly type of activity such as 'shiatsu', 'neo hypnotherapy', or 'reincarnation therapy'. No less than 844 different types of trainings and therapies are offered by the twenty-four centers that have been studied, that is no less than about thirty-five on average. This diversity on the supply side of the spiritual supermarket is illustrated by following table, that presents the 'top ten' of the most often offered types of trainings.

Table : The ten mostly offered types of trainings and therapies in 24 Dutch New Age centers (1995; N=844).

	Type of training/therapy	%
1.	Yoga	6.6
2.	Shamanism	2.6
3.	Shiatsu	2.0
4.	(Neo)reichian therapy	1.9
5.	Reiki	1.8
6.	Tarot	1.8
7.	(Neo)hypnotherapy	1.8
8.	Gestalt therapy	1.7
9.	Psychosynthesis	1.3
10.	Zen meditation	1.2
11.	Other	77.3
	Total	100.0

The ten most popular ones account for less than a quarter of the total of 844 different types of trainings and therapies on offer. The category 'other' thus captures an extreme diversity: most of those are unique for a single New Age center. This staggering diversity is caused by the tendency of New Age trainers and therapists to draw upon multiple traditions, styles, and ideas simultaneously, combining them into idiosyncratic packages. One trainer might use tarot cards in combination with crystal healing and ideas from Hinduism about chakras, whereas another might combine traditional Chinese medicine, western psychotherapy, and Taoism into another idiosyncratic concoction. This tendency was already discussed thirty-five years ago by Luckmann[31] under the label 'bricolage', a concept borrowed from Levi-Strauss. It has become a key feature of the

New Age market since. 'Standard therapies' are simply not to be found.

Nevertheless, at a higher level of generality, we can distinguish three general sources the New Age market draws upon. The first, esotericism, has already been discussed above. The second is oriental religion. No less than 29 percent of the 844 trainings and therapies offered by those 24 New Age centers rely on elements of oriental religion. Most salient among those are Hinduism (activities related to mandalas, mantras, chakras, and auras), Taoism (practices inspired by the principle of Yin and Yang), and traditional Chinese medicine (particularly healing activities that assume meridians and life energy). The third general source that the New Age centers draw upon is psychology. 'New Age religion (tends) to blur the distinction between religion and psychology to an extent hardly found in other traditions,' as Hanegraaff correctly observes[32].

Especially the work of humanist psychologist Jung 'enabled people to talk about God while really meaning their own psyche, and about their own psyche while really meaning the divine'[33]. Establishing contact with one's deeper spiritual self, and the closely connected quest for 'personal growth', borrowed from humanist psychology, then underlies the diversity of the contemporary New Age scene: '(...) "personal growth" can be understood as the shape "religious salvation" takes in the New Age Movement: it is affirmed that deliverance from human suffering and weakness will be reached by developing our human potential, which results in our increasingly getting in touch with our inner divinity'[34]. Consistent with the primacy of gnosis in esotericism, New Age rejects any belief in 'external' sources of truth and meaning. Those can only be found within the deeper layers of the self: '(...) the most pervasive and significant aspect of the lingua franca of the New Age is that the person is, in essence, spiritual. To experience the "Self" itself is to experience "God", "the Goddess", the "Source", "Christ

Consciousness", the "inner child", the "way of the heart", or, most simply and (...) most frequently, "inner spirituality"[35].

Despite the enormous diversity on the shelves of the late-modern spiritual supermarket, in short, the courses, trainings, and therapies on offer have a common objective, that is too easily overlooked by observers who merely acknowledge the syncretism and volatility of the New Age scene. This common objective, that constitutes the defining characteristic of New Age, is the (re-)establishment of contact with the spiritual self, that is held to have become overgrown with the weeds of socialization (the socialized self or 'ego'). The range of trainings and therapies offered by New Age centers stimulates and assists their New Age clients to reach beyond the ego and once again experience the 'real self' as the only valid source of meaning and identity.

3. Sacralizing the Self and Demonizing Institutions

3.1. The Primacy of Self-Spirituality

Recent research among trainers of Dutch New Age centers confirms the primacy of gnosis and self-spirituality[36]. 'What is faith?,' one of the respondents asks, immediately giving the characteristic answer himself: 'Something that one takes for granted. Just like that. Faith is (...) a limitation.' All other respondents come up with similar ideas. They criticize faith and the churches, thus primarily critiquing established dogmas, rules and ideas:

I think the churches failed above all because 'expressing it from within oneself' (...) has totally got lost. It got lost in two ways. The first way is that it has become a system of rules, dogmas (...) the second is that it has been intellectualized. It has become brains only. (respondent 8, male)

(In) a church, as we know it anyway, the stories have already been worked out (and one has) some sort of pre-determined role of how it should be done. How one should live. But I prefer to find my own source and to determine from my own source what is my conscience and how I would like to live. (respondent 9, female)

Hence, our respondents indicate that Christian dogmas, rituals, and moral rules preclude self-spirituality and personal growth. Traditional Christians, one declares, 'are imprisoned in the lard of the dogmas.' Spirituality is instead held to reside within the deeper layers of the self: 'I experience (…) the Divine as something inside myself (...) It is all about self-knowledge and self-awareness,' 'I consider spirituality something that lives inside myself, ' and 'I am God myself. (…) I am going to feel!'

Theologist Tom Beaudoin[37] nicely captures this feature of post-Christian religiosity in the chapter titles 'Institutions Are Suspect' and 'Experience Is Key' of his book *Virtual Faith* (1998). Being the long-standing western religious institution, it is hardly surprising that criticism is primarily directed at the Christian church. It applies to other religious traditions and new religious movements, too, however. One respondent remarks about the movement of Baghwan (or 'Osho'), for instance:

On the one hand it has a lot of flexibility and freedom, but it too has norms and values (…) People go and change their names. Yes, that is supposed to be very valuable… That doesn't appeal to me very much. (…) In every current there is an underlying danger of norms and values coming to dominate and limit personal liberty. (respondent 10, female)

New Agers do not simply oppose the substantial ideas of Christianity, Islam, and other traditional religions, then. They rather oppose the exerted institutional pressure, because this leaves insufficient room for personal spiritual experience ('gnosis').

3.2. Simply Becoming Who One Is

This resistance to institutional pressure is underscored by our respondents' opposition to non-religious institutions and the social roles tied to them. Social roles are rejected because our respondents want to 'be themselves' under all circumstances and do not want to play 'unnatural' roles, considered inconsistent with their 'true selves'. They strongly feel that one should not behave in a particular way because 'everybody expects one to act that way,' but simply because one 'feels like it.' The following remarks about traditional gender roles illustrate this:

I don't want to behave according to a certain gender role, because I want to be myself at all times. I think that if one can't be oneself, one definitely cannot or will not feel good in oneself. (respondent 2, female)

If it is forced onto one by society, 'This is how one should behave as a woman,' then that is all very nice; it gives one a sense of social security, because 'I do it well according to society.' But later on, one becomes more conscious and one thinks: 'Yes, but do I actually want this?' (...) One can choose oneself. Isn't that much nicer than when the world, society, chooses on one's behalf? (respondent 5, male)

As soon as (...) society or whatever forces me into a certain role, it may feel unnatural. Because I have to play a role that is not really me. (respondent 7, male)

In the same way our respondents reject the idea that marriage as an institution, i.e., apart from the well being of the individual spouses, has a right to exist and deserves protection and preservation. 'If one gets the feeling that one restrains oneself,' one respondent states, 'then that's a reason for divorce.' Another respondent even goes a step further by stating: 'Marriage is essentially merely an annoying obstacle to getting divorced.' This ideal of personal authenticity has an interesting theoretical consequence that deserves some special attention. It means that the display of behavior that is consistent with traditional roles does not necessarily indicate traditional action in Max Weber's[38] classical sense.

This is especially visible in the case of traditional gender roles. Some of the women explain that they have deliberately stopped working and become full-time mothers when their children were young. They did not make this decision because traditional gender roles expected them to do so, but because they experience motherhood as 'natural' and fulfilling. In her recent book on post-feminist ideologies of motherhood, Bobel[39] refers to this as 'natural mothering.' 'Natural mothers' are suspicious of dominant institutions and criticize liberal feminism as privileging rather than weakening masculine dominance. Instead, as an act of cultural resistance, they sacralize the bond between mother and child and insist on the existence of natural differences between male and female experience. Women and motherhood are even more explicitly linked by our New Age respondents, because of the typical valuation of 'the feminine' in New Age circles – by men as well as women. This glorification of femininity in New Agecircles tends to go hand in hand with a reproduction of the traditional inequality between the sexes[40]. 'At least you knew where you stood with straightforward chauvinists,' a female New Ager cited by Prince and Riches[41] cynically remarks in this context.

Beliefs and values relating to the bringing up of children further confirm New Age's anti-institutionalism. The external imposition of parental norms and values upon children is forcefully rejected. Our respondents argue that children should only be encouraged to 'simply become who they are,' as is demonstrated by their claims about the main goal of parental socialization:

To accompany, so that the personality of the child can fully come out. To make sure that the child can be himself, with all of his craziness, particularities. I think that is very important. (respondent 10, female)

That they can become who they are. That is the final aim: to just become who one is. (respondent 6, female)

I think one can mean most to children by just showing them life. That is, without influencing them. (respondent 1, male)

The anti-church and anti-Christian sentiments among New Agers, in short, are merely elements of a more general 'anti-institutional mood'[42].

3.3. Functional Rationality: Buildings, Desks, and Boxes

This generalized anti-institutionalism is also confirmed by the way our respondents judge specialized modern occupational roles and functional rationality. They are distinctly negative about bureaucracy and processes of bureaucratization. Bureaucratic rules and organizational forms are regarded 'alienating', 'nonsensical', 'inhumane', and 'unanimated.' They refer to bureaucrats disapprovingly as 'people who sit in buildings to invent rules' and 'people sitting behind desks and (...) inventing plans without knowing what really happens on the work floor.' 'Bureaucracy does not work anymore. (...) People are no more willing to play this game,' a respondent argues. The formalized character of bureaucracy is held to prevent its employees and clients from 'simply being themselves': it misunderstands what makes them into unique individuals, destroys inspiration and animation, and forces people to stop and think for themselves, effectively numbing them in the process. Every individual human being is unique, or so our respondents argue, and hence work needs to offer opportunities for expressing this individuality. 'I very much believe that people should be there where they belong,' one respondent remarks in this context. Working under rationalized relations is, in short, depicted as 'unanimated', 'inhumane', and fatal for opportunities for personal growth.

Very much like we have seen in our discussion of the possibility of voluntarily and self-consciously choosing for patterns of conduct that resemble 'traditional action' for the superficial external observer, our respondents reject the idea that such a thing as a 'transpersonal' point of view exists, that could be used to 'objectively' judge the quality of work. In this case, too, it is only personal experience that is decisive. 'It's just an assumption that work is alienating,' one respondent explains, arguing that 'alienation is merely a concept.' As a consequence, he appends, alienation is not the inevitable outcome of working under rationalized relations, but essentially an individual choice, too:

> One can choose to alienate from things around one. But that's also a choice. Because one can also say: 'I keep my attention with it. I see it as some sort of meditation. I keep my attention with my work. I do it with one hundred percent of dedication.' Then it becomes a sort of Zen-meditation. Then it's not alienating. Then one comes very close to oneself. (respondent 7, male)

Hence, whether or not rationalized work is 'alienating' and 'obstructing self-actualization' is not given by its 'objective' characteristics. What is alienating and numbing for one person, might actually be liberating for another by offering excellent opportunities for making contact with the 'spiritual self.' Some people, for instance, even indulge themselves in work that many others find alienating:

> Some people love that! There are people who love to be surrounded by rules and to execute rules and to point out a comma to others. 'You can't do that! Here is that comma!' (respondent 5, male)

Apart from resistance to functional rationality as an externally imposed characteristic of modern work organizations, we also find a more general distrust of the modern primacy of reasoning, categorizing, and conceptualizing. This rationalist bias is held to leave no room for personal experience and as such to disregard individual differences. Because every single person is unique, rationally invented standards never cover multifarious reality; they are nothing but artificial constructs:

> I am opposed to all concepts. (...) A concept for me is

adjusting to what is already there. Why don't you develop something totally new? You are an entirely new person! (respondent 9, female)

One cannot motivate two persons in the same way. The motivation of persons to do or not do something is entirely different. For one it is this, for the other it is this, for yet another it is that. (respondent 5, male)

Subjecting people to rationally informed classifications – 'Sorting everything neatly into boxes. Then it is safe' – is denounced, then, as a dismal and unproductive practice: 'Neither children nor adults belong in boxes. (…) I am not a box. That is not possible'; 'Why should we put (people) in a box? I think everyone should be able to live as one wishes'.

4. 'Institutions Make One Sick'

The quest for self-spirituality and the sacralization of the self, our data demonstrate, gives rise to a demonizing of institutions. Everything that is not self-chosen, but 'artificially' and 'externally' imposed, and that as such subordinates the self to pre-given patterns of behavior, is rejected. Such a resistance against institutional pressure was expressed time and again during the interviews in more general ways, too:

Imposing things from the outside, I am totally opposed to that anyway. That doesn't tally with finding one's own way in life and experiencing what is good for me. (respondent 4, female)

I am actually totally opposed to everything that is prescribed. Because I just want to create things from within myself. (…) Every authority that imposes itself as authority restricts the development of a personal, inner authority. (respondent 9, female)

It is of course not only faith and church, but actually our whole Christian culture, our Western culture, which (…) with all kinds of explicit or implicit taboos (…) impairs self-actualization. (respondent 8, male)

The characterization of institutions as essentially alienating is, in short, indissolubly linked to the sacralization of the self: people should liberate themselves from external influences and choose authentically for what is Good, True, or Pure. What happens, then, if people adjust to institutions after all? Our respondents make many, often dramatic, pronouncements about this. Adjustment to traditional institutions and functional role expectations can work out well for quite a while, they believe, but eventually it inevitably produces problems:

I think that if one can't put anything of oneself in one's work (...) one doesn't go to work with pleasure. One often thinks negatively and that's not good for oneself. It makes one ill, both physically and mentally. (respondent 2, female)

It can make many people ill. You should only know how many people have mental and psychosomatic complaints, because they find themselves in a social role where they don't belong. One comes across such persons regularly in this center. (respondent 5, male)

About the consequences of too much of an identification with the work role:

'I am my work.' I hear that often. People who retire and fall into a black hole. 'I don't exist anymore. I am my work, my status. I am an executive. And tomorrow it is "Goodbye!" and nobody calls me anymore.' That's tough. And then it goes wrong. Such a person will become bitter. Become unhappy. Sometimes they will die very soon. So, 'I exist less.' Which is absolutely untrue. (...) One always exists. (respondent 1, male)

In bringing up children there is the same danger. A traditional, authoritarian upbringing, forcefully rejected by our respondents, inevitably results in 'a sense of inferiority, insecurity, effacing oneself, and believing that another person is more than he or she is.' Too directive an upbringing is thus held to cause mental and emotional damage to children:

One shouldn't program in advance how one wants a child to become. That's how many children get screwed up. They will end up in mental health care. Just because the parents emphasize too much how they want the child to develop. (respondent 5, male)

Frustrations about institutional adjustment are held to lead not only to problems of mental and physical health, but to violent types of crime, too:

One does not live brilliantly anymore. One holds back, watches out, pays attention to not make a mistake. One is busy doing that, instead of being natural. And that can come out distortedly in all kinds of ways. That someone really develops a sick mind. Crimes can result from that. (respondent 9, female).

Repressing sexual desire, 'as encouraged by the church,' also has undesirable results, according to this respondent: 'If physical tension cannot be released through sexuality, they have to arrange something else. Or they get a heart attack.' And she adds:

If one is flowing naturally, you can see that in small children and in animals, then everything makes sense. Then it just makes sense how one lives. (...) And if in one way or another this flow gets stemmed, then it is just like a brook that flows down from a mountain. Then the water has to come out one way or another. And then it can come out in very different ways. Often very ugly ways. (...) If one knows what one is doing, then one can make choices, and one can deal with it, one can handle as big a force as sexuality. (...) Whereas if one doesn't really know that that force is present within one, but comes to expression in a different way, then all kinds of sick things are the result. Like child pornography and stuff like that. (respondent 9, female)

Adjustment to institutional role expectations, to sum up, is regarded a principal source of personal and social problems by our respondents. They attribute frustrations, bitterness, unhappiness, mental disorders, depressions, but also physical diseases, spontaneous violent outbursts, and indulgence in sick forms of sexuality to a state of alienation from the spiritual self. And this alienation is considered the inescapable result of adjustment to institutional role expectations. 'Institutions make one sick,' their dramatic message reads.

5. Whence this 20th -Century Turn to the Self?

New Age's radical individualism is in flat contradiction with the arguably most fundamental sociological assumption: that to lead a more or less satisfactory human life, people need to sacrifice the satisfaction of their most primary impulses and desires. This is not only the central message of the work of sociologists such as Durkheim, Elias, and Parsons, but also of Freud's[43]. In a polemical critique of the latter's essay *Civilization and its Discontents* (1961), Bauman[44] rightly argues that today the exact opposite is happening[45]. People are becoming less willing to repress their deepest longings and instincts. They are increasingly prepared to sacrifice institutional regulation to the quest for individual liberty, self-expression, and personal happiness. This is exemplified by today's 'numerous "self-improvement" movements, deriving their seductive power from the promise of developing the sensuous potential of the body through exercise, contemplation, self-concentration, breaking psychic blocks and convention-induced constraints, letting free the suppressed instincts (...)'[46].

This quest for self-spirituality in the West is easily misconstrued as a 'regression' to 'premodern irrationality', but we are in fact dealing with a radically modern phenomenon (see especially Heelas 1996). It entails a radicalization of the ethics of authenticity that has accompanied modernity from its very beginnings[47]. The modern sensitivity to the self is a logical outgrowth of the process of rationalization that has increasingly undermined the possibility of finding 'objective' meaning in the external world. Because of their increasing formalization, abstraction, and differentiation, modern institutions lose their ability to provide the self with meaning. As a result, the modern self increasingly experiences itself as separated from the institutional order – no longer as a 'natural' or 'organic' part of it, as in pre-modern society, but rather as facing it 'from the outside', as it were[48]. 'Modern man has suffered from a deepening condition of "homelessness",' Berger et al.[49] explain: 'The correlate of his experience of society and of self has been what might be called a metaphysical loss of "home" (...) It has therefore engendered its own nostalgias – nostalgias, that is, for a condition of "being at home" in society, with oneself and, ultimately, in the universe'.

With the unfolding of the process of rationalization, institutions have become unmasked as merely human inventions without solid metacultural foundations. It has become widely felt that they might as well have been 'different' and accordingly they no longer enjoy the levels of 'self-evidence' and 'reality' they were traditionally endowed with. What happens in such a radically disenchanted type of society that no longer provides the self with pre-given meaning and that as such inevitably brings forth problems of meaning and identity? What happens if the self, thrown back upon itself, becomes immersed in nagging questions such as 'Who am I *really* as a person?' or 'What do I *really* want'? Taking refuge in a postmodern sense of irony and contingency is not going to bring one very far if one feels that questions such as those need to be answered in a solid and personally convincing way. Under those circumstances one necessarily clutches at the straw of the self as the only remaining personally convincing source of meaning. One embarks for a voyage of discovery to the deeper layers of the self to search for 'real' meaning and 'real' identity there and thus re-infuse life with new meaning and purpose.

In quite a paradoxical way, to sum up, problems of meaning and identity, produced by the process of rationalization and the disenchantment of the world that accompanies it, constitute the starting point for a reenchantment of the western world. It is important to underline that this is indeed a process of reenchantment rather than a sort of regression to premodern belief systems. The sacred is, after all, no longer believed to be found in the external world, but rather within the deeper layers of the self. New Age's sacralization of the self in contemporary western societies is then the paradoxical apotheosis of the modern preoccupation with the self, produced by the processes of rationalization and disenchantment.

6. Conclusion: New Age and Oriental Religion

The religious landscapes of western societies have changed dramatically during the last few decades. In most of them, the Christian churches have declined considerably, whereas New Age as a post-traditional type of religion has remarkably increased during this same period[50]. As a corollary to this increased interest in New Age, oriental religions are more salient in the west today than they have ever been before. Although there is no denying that western culture deeply affects the rest of the globe, forcing non-western societies to either passively adapt to western lifestyles and aspirations or actively react to them in more or less militant ways, that is certainly not all that is taking place. The remarkably increased interest in oriental religious ideas and practices in today's western societies is one of the key examples of such a movement in the opposite direction.

The fascination for the east in the modern west cannot be denounced as merely a patronizing type of 'orientalism', reflecting and reinforcing western feelings of cultural superiority[51]. Such a view ignores the extent to which much of today's fascination with oriental religion in the New Age circuit in the west stems from the cultural discontents produced by the twin processes of rationalization and disenchantment. The orient is constructed as 'a timeless place that transcends the problems of this world, a place where the West can escape from its ills, a place where the West can seek peaceful solace'[52]. The current fascination with the east in western societies, in short, arises from a self-critical appraisal of the west as much as from an approving, although stereotypical, image of the east as having fostered for centuries the spirituality that has, in the west itself, not simply been lost, but effectively destroyed (see also Clarke[53] as cited by Lau)[54].

Today's interest in oriental religion in the western world has been produced by the largely endogenous western processes of rationalization and disenchantment, then, that have eventually cut off all possibilities to find meaning in the world external to the self. We are dealing with one of those wonderful ironies of history here. The very religious traditions that long ago, according to Max Weber[55], obstructed the rationalization of the oriental world, are today embraced in western attempts to infuse life with new meaning, now that the old belief systems have been destroyed by the process of rationalization that the western world once provided with fertile soil.

Notes and References

1. Benjamin R. Barber, *Jihad vs. McWorld*, New York: Times Books, 1995.
2. Samuel P. Huntington, *The Clash of Civilizations and the Remaking of World Order*, New York: Simon & Schuster, 1996.
3. Kimberly J. Lau, *New Age Capitalism: Making Money East of Eden*, Philadelphia: University of Pennsylvania Press, 2000.
4. The authors wish to acknowledge the invaluable support of Inge van der Tak during the collection of the data analyzed in sections 3 and 4 of this paper (compare Aupers et al. 2003). Please direct all correspondence to: Stef Aupers, Department of Sociology, Faculty of Social Sciences, Erasmus University, P.O. Box 1738, 3000 DR Rotterdam, the Netherlands (email: Aupers@fsw.eur.nl).
5. The esoterical tradition is influenced by premodern

traditions like gnosticism and neoplatonism (e.g., Wichmann 1990), but started – according to Hanegraaff (1996) with the translation of the so-called *Corpus Hermeticum* in 1462 or 1463 by the scholar Marcello Ficino; also see, *The Perennial Philosophy* by Aldous Huxley (1994 [1945]).

6. Wouter Hanegraaff, *New Age Religion and Western Culture: Esotericism in the Mirror of Secular Thought*, Leiden: Brill, 1996.
7. Wouter Hanegraaff, Ibid., note 6.
8. Despite this continuity, Blavatsky made a fundamental change by transforming the religious 'perennial view' into a testable scientific hypothesis. By encouraging the comparative study of religion she thus eventually hoped to find a scientific basis for the esoterical idea that all religions are valid.
9. Paul Heelas, *The New Age Movement*. Oxford: Blackwell, 1996.
10. Wouter Hanegraaff, Ibid., note 6.
11. Wouter Hanegraaff, Ibid., note 6.
12. Wouter Hanegraaff, Ibid., note 6.
13. Wichmann, Jörg *Die Renaissance der Esoterik: Eine kritische Orientierung*, Stuttgart: Kreuz, 1990.
14. Wouter Hanegraaff, Ibid., note 6.
15. Anton C. Zijderveld, *The Abstract Society: A Cultural Analysis of Our Time*, Garden City, N.Y. : Doubleday, 1970.
16. Elizabeth Puttick, "Personal Development: The Spiritualisation and Secularisation of the Human Potential Movement" in Steven Sutcliffe and Marion Bowman (eds.), *Beyond New Age: Exploring Alternative Spirituality*, Edinburgh: Edinburgh University Press, 2000, pp. 201-219.
17. T. Roszak, *The Making of a Counter Culture: Reflections on*

the Technocratic Society and Its Youthful Opposition, Garden City, N.Y. : Doubleday, 1969.

18. Miranda Moerland and Anneke van Otterloo, "New Age: Tegencultuur, paracultuur of kerncultuur?" ["New Age: Counter Culture, Para-Culture, or Nuclear Culture?"], *Amsterdams Sociologisch Tijdschrift*, 1996, 23 (4), pp. 682-710.
19. Anneke Van Otterloo, "Selfspirituality and the Body: New Age Centres in The Netherlands since the 1960s", *Social Compass*, 1999, 46 (2), pp. 191-202.
20. Van Otterloo, Ibid., note 19.
21. Steven Sutcliffe and Marion Bowman, "Introduction" in Steven Sutcliffe and Marion Bowman (eds.), *Beyond New Age: Exploring Alternative Spirituality*, Edinburgh: Edinburgh University Press, 2000, pp. 1-13.
22. Paul Heelas, Ibid., note 9.
23. Elizabeth Puttick, Ibid., note 16.
24. Adam Possamai, "Alternative Spiritualities and the Cultural Logic of Late Capitalism", *Culture and Religion*, 2003, 4 (1), pp. 31-45.
25. Thomas Luckmann, *The Invisible Religion*, London: MacMillan, 1967.
26. Van Otterloo, "Anneke Moderne spiritualiteit en secularisatie" ["Modern spirituality and secularization"] in Bart Voorsluis (ed.) *Moderne spiritualiteit tussen traditie en vernieuwing [Modern Spirituality between Tradition and Renewal]*, Zoetermeer: Meinema, 1997, pp. 13-25.
27. Paul Schnabel, *Tussen stigma en charisma: Nieuwe religieuze bewegingen en geestelijke volksgezondheid [Between Stigma and Charisma: New Religious Movements and Mental Health Care]*, Deventer: Van Loghum Slaterus, 1982.
28. Kimberly J. Lau, Ibid note 3.
29. Rodney Stark and William Sims Bainbridge, *The Future of*

Religion: Secularization, Revival, and Cult Formation, Berkeley: University of California Press, 1985.

30. Stef Aupers, "Werken aan lichaam, emoties en energie in New Age-centra: Een 'hertovering'?" ["Working on Body, Emotions and Energy in New Age Centers: A 'Reenchantment'?"], *Sociologische Gids,* 2000, 47(5), pp. 350-65.
31. Michel Maffesoli, Ibid., note 15.
32. Wouter Hanegraaff, Ibid., note 6.
33. Wouter Hanegraaff, Ibid., note 6.
34. Wouter Hanegraaff, Ibid., note 6.
35. Paul Heelas, Ibid., note 9.
36. Stef Aupers, Dick Houtman and Inge van der Tak, "Gewoon worden wie je bent : Over authenticiteit en anti-institutionalisme" ["Simply Becoming You Are': On Authenticity and Anti-Institutionalism"], *Sociologische Gids,* 2003, 50 (2), pp. 203-223.
37. Tom Beaudoin, *Virtual Faith: The Irreverent Spiritual Quest of Generation X,* San Francisco: Jossey Bass, 1998.
38. Max Weber, *Economy and Society (Two Volumes),* Berkeley/ Los Angeles: University of California Press, 1978 [1921].
39. Chris Bobel, *The Paradox of Natural Mothering,* Philadelphia, PA: Temple University, 2002.
40. Bobel also emphasizes the way the glorification of 'the feminine' by 'natural mothers' serves to leave the traditional inequality between the sexes intact, reproducing rather than challenging it.
41. Ruth Prince and David Riches, *The New Age in Glastonbury: The Construction of Religious Movements,* New York/Oxford: Berghahn Books, 2000.
42. Anton C. Zijderveld, *The Institutional Imperative: The*

Interface of Institutions and Networks, Amsterdam: Amsterdam University Press, 2000.

43. Sigmund Freud, *Civilization and Its Discontents*, New York: W.W. Norton & Company, 1961 [1930].

44. Bauman Zygmunt, *Postmodernity and Its Discontents*, Cambridge: Polity Press, 1997.

45. Michel Maffesoli, *The Time of the Tribes: The Decline of Individualism in Mass Society*, London: Sage, 1996.

46. Bauman Zygmunt, Ibid., note 44.

47. Lionel Trilling, *Sincerity and Authenticity*, Cambridge, MA: Harvard University Press, 1974; and Charles Taylor, *The Ethics of Authenticity*, Cambridge, MA : Harvard University Press, 1992.

48. Arnold Gehlen, *Man in the Age of Technology*, New York: Columbia University Press, 1980 [1957]; and T. Roszak, Ibid., note 17.

49. Peter L. Berger, Brigitte Berger and Hansfried Kellner, *The Homeless Mind: Modernization and Consciousness*, New York: Random House, 1973.

50. Dick Houtman and Peter Mascini, "Why Do Churches Become Empty, While New Age Grows? Secularization and Religious Change in the Netherlands", *Journal for the Scientific Study of Religion*, 2002, 41 (3), pp. 455-473.

51. Said, Edward W. *Orientalism*, New York: Pantheon, 1978.

52. Kimberly J. Lau, Ibid., note 3.

53. J.J. Clarke, *Oriental Enlightenment: The Encounter between Asian and Western Thought*, London: Routledge, 1997.

54. Kimberly J. Lau, Ibid., note 3.

55. Max Weber, *The Sociology of Religion*, Boston: Beacon Press, 1963 [1922].

****

5

The Sweatshop as an Element of National Development : China as a Case in Point

*Joseph M. Conforti**

1. Introduction

If the opportunity to exploit workers through sweatshops may be expected to be a common part of national development, examples of which are replete in history, the anti-sweatshop movement of the past decade has nevertheless focused particular attention on the role that sweatshops have played and continue to play in the exceptional development of China. This poses the question of whether sweatshops in China simply reflect the early industrialization of another developing country, or if there are factors in China's development that would make it especially likely to generate sweatshops in the course of its industrial development. In the course of its recent development China has been going through a set of social and economic transitions that can only be characterized as extraordinary (Chow Kong Wing and Fung Ka Yiu[1]; Demurger et. al.[2]; Duckett[3]; Gibb and Li[4]). The sheer size of the country's population, of course, makes any change there somewhat unique. That its industrial development is occurring largely in the form of free enterprise capitalism in an ostensibly socialist country, tightly ruled by the Communist Party, in a context of

* Department of Sociology State University of New York, Old Westbury, Box 210, Old Westbury, NY 11568-0210

global capitalism, makes it even more unique. That China is, furthermore, a relatively conservative society, makes the pace and scope of these changes more striking still.

It is not entirely unique, however. There are some broad parallels to the Industrial Revolution experienced earlier in the Western world, such as the simultaneous growth and spread of industrialization and urbanization. Some of the forms of industrialization are also very similar to the early stages of the Western world's Industrial Revolution, particularly the development of sweatshops. That sweatshops would develop in the early stages of industrialization, is not in itself surprising. Until legislation establishing rules and regulations for manufacturing activities are enacted and enforced, in combination with concerns for and the protection of workers' rights, it may be expected that the earliest industrial entrepreneurs and their financial backers will in any developing country seek to exploit every available opportunity to maximize profits. Insofar as the government is inevitably a direct or indirect beneficiary of such efforts to maximize profits it is also, therefore, a party to such exploitation.

When sweatshops emerged in the course of early industrialization in Europe it was in a context of family-owned and financed small businesses in the developing towns in otherwise agricultural societies. This was a new phenomenon, based upon family capitalization, occurring in a high degree of isolation, at a time when rules and regulations, concern for the health, safety or the welfare of workers were essentially unknowns. One of the striking aspects of the Chinese instance is that such sweatshops have developed and seem to flourish in the peculiar context of a combination of foreign investment and severe foreign criticism, often emanating from the same countries. The criticism, coming from many parts of the world, has focused on the horrific conditions under which a mostly young female workforce is said to labour. The conditions include some of the lowest pay scales found anywhere, very harsh supervision, a general lack of safety and sanitation, brutal and arduous work schedules, a denial of privacy, and a severe restriction of freedom (Chan and Senser[5]). Reports from many quarters are replete with descriptions of young women working in factories for as much as 15 to 20 hours a day, for six or seven days a week for as little as 5 cents an hour and then being locked in company-operated dormitories overnight (Kristof and WuDunn[6]; Lee[7]). All of these conditions are further aggravated by the fact that the Chinese government seems to do little, if anything, to rectify them. In fact, the Chinese government has largely refused to acknowledge the existence of such conditions (Ash[8]; National Labour Committee[9]; O' Rourke[10]).

While these conditions are unquestionably deplorable by any moral measure, and the workers in these plants are paying an unconsciousably high cost, where there are costs there are usually benefits, as is the case here. But it is also commonly the case that when the distribution of specific economic costs and benefits in a society are weighed, it is not the same people who pay the costs and reap the benefits. Obviously, if workers are being exploited in sweatshops, those who own the sweatshops, those who have directly or indirectly invested in the sweatshops, and those who buy the products of the sweatshops all benefit. Such beneficiaries would be located both within China and beyond. This is very much in keeping with the familiar criticisms that Marx and Engels leveled at early industrial capitalism in the West, largely criticisms of an exploitative bourgeoisie (Marx[11]).

In the capitalistic industrialization of the West in the early to mid 19th Century an exploitative bourgeoisie was a far simpler phenomenon than it is today, particularly in places like China, that are part of a newly globalized and far more complex capitalism. In the 19th Century West the patrimonial organization of small scale industry merged the owner, manager, product designer, financier and marketer in a single family, if not a single entrepreneur. Today this involves a vastly more intricate set of relationships among a set of entities throughout the world. The factories are still likely to be small in scale and patrimonial. But everything else about them tends to determined by forces far afield. The commodities they produce are defined by tastes and markets elsewhere, as are all the properties of those commodities. Insofar as the sweatshops in China are often sub-contractors of sub-contractors, they may never even produce a whole product. Rather, they may be producing components or parts of components in an elaborate global division of labour that ultimately eventuates in a finished product. It might very well be the case that they do not even know what the ultimate product will be.

2. The Chinese Road to Capitalism

The conditions under which this form of industrialization originated in China need to be taken into consideration in order to better understand the form it has taken. That the earliest conditions were mostly illegal, or extra legal, undermines any opportunity to document them, though the conditions are quite relevant to understanding the development of sweat shops in southeastern China. The origins probably go back decades in relation to Hong Kong in particular, and if to a lesser degree, to Taiwan as well.

In the post World War II period the economy of Hong Kong flourished. That Hong Kong had become a financial and trade center in this period is well recognized and well reflected in a skyline comprised of hi-rise banks, corporate and financial offices. Less well reflected, however, was Hong Kong's industrial base, comprised largely of very small manufacturing companies located in obscure small facilities that accommodated few employees, and even less space for manufacturing equipment (Ho[12]; Lau[13]). This was apparently one of the activities in space-starved Hong Kong that could not be accommodated in skyscrapers, except perhaps for some of their workers who did piece work at home in their apartments. These activities could be further accommodated, however, if extralegally, in the extraterritorial areas of neighboring Guangdong province. Thus, in many cases, their employees, the equipment and all the other facilities needed to manufacture the goods that the Hong Kong entrepreneurs sold were actually located across the border in mainland China. It is certainly not surprising that when the Chinese government decided to establish Special Economic Zones in 1979, the first and foremost location of the zones was (and still is) in Guangdong province adjacent to Hong Kong (and neighboring Fujian Province). In many respects the establishment of the Special Economic Zones served only to legalize and extend a structure already largely in place. This meant that prior to Hong Kong's return to Chinese jurisdiction in 1997 the nascent industrial development of Southeast China was already joined to the well established trade and financial facilities of Hong Kong, and thereby to the rest of the world, in a mutually beneficial division of labour (Chan, et. al.[14]; Tuan and Ng[15]).

These developments occurred in a global context of shifting industrial production. The United States and Western Europe were going through a post industrial transition, while Japan, later joined by Korea and other industrializing Asian countries, was expanding its share of worldwide manufacturing activity. Initially a war-devastated and occupied Japan offered an abundance of workers desperate for employment who could be exploited by American companies through subsidiary Japanese employers. The American companies could then shift some of their manufacturing activities to Japan, offering the Japanese workers much lower wages than they had been paying to their American workers. Given Japan's own recent industrial experience, however, it was able to capitalize upon this manufacturing activity to rapidly develop a substantial industrial base of its own. Over the next half century, however, with a finite labour force, Japan's workers increasingly priced themselves out of competition, and industrial production increasingly shifted to South Korea, Taiwan, Thailand and other Southeast Asian nations. Like Japan, while many of them began as subcontractors and subsidiaries of foreign companies, some went on to develop their own substantial industrial bases. Inevitably, these nations would in turn begin to price themselves out of labour competition, opening opportunities for any nation in the region that was in a position to provide flexible production facilities with abundant cheap labour, and no country was in a better position to do that than China (Yifu, Cai and Lee[16]). And, within China, no area was in a better position to do so than Guangdong Province.

That such industrial development is still largely limited to the Special Economic Zones underscores the degree to which China is not a capitalist society. It would hardly meet the criteria delineated by Weber[17] almost a century ago. It is likely, however, that the success of the Special Economic Zones will generate an expansion of their capitalism to comprise an ever larger portion of the Chinese economy.

3. Underlying Factors

In looking at the factors underlying the development of sweatshops in China there has to be taken into consideration the interaction of several factors that challenge, if not defy, the logic of their mutual fit. Economic reform is fundamental to the emergence, but to "...cultivate and develop a socialist market economy..." seems a clear contradiction in terms (Guoguang[18]). In fact, much of the economic reform in China contains contradictory strains (Hou and Hou[19]).

Reforms in agriculture, for example, increased production and reduced labour input, thus freeing up millions of people from agriculture to move to industrial jobs in urban areas. But neither the central government nor local governments provide any facilitation of such movement. While the industrialization of China's East Coast has been the main basis of China's modern economic development, and therefore a likely permanent site of industry in any foreseeable future, the millions of people who have moved there to staff the factories are defined as a *temporary population* or a *floating population* (Seeborg, Jin and Zhu[20]; Shen[21]).

This *temporary* population is routinely denied the rights and opportunities available to the *permanent* urban population in such areas as housing, education, medical services and welfare. The contradictory dimension here lies in the accommodating role that the workplace had played in China since 1949 as not only the source of income, but also a variety of essential social services such as housing, education and health care (Leung[22]). As a result, this population is simultaneously a critically important component in China's economic development and a discvalued group of second-class citizens treated with contempt. This underscores several related factors underlying the emergence of sweatshops in China. Relative to demand, the supply of such *temporary* urbanites is almost infinite in size. Together with their numbers, their second-class citizen status makes them all but dispensable, and certainly exploitable. Employers do not have to concern themselves with the loss of such workers since they are so readily replaceable. Given their exploitative wages, the workers usually have no choice but to live in factory dormitories since little or no other housing is affordable to them. When to these circumstances, there is added the practices of many factory employers' holding workers' identity papers and the first month's wages, the workers might well be described as being in a state of semi-slavery (Ash[23]; Chan and Senser[24]; Shen[25]).

In fairness to the employers, it should be noted here that the workers coming to the factories from rural areas in the North are highly unskilled and untrained and therefore prone to low productivity, to making mistakes and causing accidents (Foster[26]). The resulting wastage raises production costs and accounts, at least in part, for the low wages and intense supervision in the factories. In keeping with the contradictory strains, Foster[27] also points out that such workers from the rural North are nevertheless preferred over the local Cantonese workers from Guangdong who are regarded as lazy and dishonest.

Similar to the labour supply generated by agricultural reform, another if lesser (but potentially expansive) supply of labour has been generated by reform in state owned enterprises. This has occurred largely through the encouragement of competition and the loosening of regulations (Wang and Chang[28]). State owned enterprises have been highly inefficient, including among their inefficiencies the retention of larger numbers of workers on their payrolls than are actually needed. Given the increase in competition and decreased government support, these companies are subject to abrupt bankruptcy closure, displacing large numbers of workers with little compensation and little recourse (Wong and Kinglun[29]). Less drastically, some state owned enterprises, under pressure to increase efficiency, may simply dismiss redundant employees that they had been carrying on the company payroll, a common practice that Wong and Kinglun[30] call *hidden unemployment*.

Whatever the basis of their availability, employees released from state owned enterprises are likely to be permanent urban residents. Their unemployment is likely to place them in direct competition with the temporary urban population, to the further disadvantage of the latter (Seeborg, Jin and Zhu[31]).

If the enormous number of workers available to the sweatshops from various sources can be thought of as a labor *supply,* then there is also a complex of underlying factors that might be said to constitute the *demand* for such labour. One such factor would go back to 1978, in terms of the economic stagnation that served as a broad context for the reforms of that period, particularly following the disastrous Cultural Revolution.

Beyond the reforms in agriculture, the hoped for development of China's economy had to be influenced by the dramatic experience of Japan's industrial development and that of the smaller Southeast Asian nations such as South Korea, Thailand and Singapore (Harding[32]). In conjunction with the Hong Kong-Guangdong manufacturing nexus, and perhaps a similar but smaller Taiwan-Fujian nexus, this inevitably meant manufacturing for export. Of course, it also meant that China would have to compete with Japan and the other Southeast Asian nations in its manufacturing for export, in terms of quality, cost and flexibility. If quality might have been an initial shortcoming in China's competitive stance, it was more than offset by cost and flexibility.

The kind of small-scale manufacturing that originated in Southeastern China in relation to Hong Kong, now comprising much of the Special Economic Zones' production, was particularly well-suited to meeting this kind of competition. That China could possibly have attracted foreign capital investment under other circumstances is highly unlikely. Few foreign investors would likely risk their capital in large-scale ventures in a socialist country tightly controlled by a Communist Party historically dedicated to central planning and state ownership of all major economic facilities. But small-scale ventures, requiring relatively small investments, were worth risking. In aggregate, such small-scale investments became a large-scale foreign investment in China (Chen, Chang and Zhang[33]; Fung, Iizaka and Parker[34]). In turn, the increasing volume of foreign investment became a major factor in the demand for more and more sweatshop labour.

The foreign capital flowing into China, while a force in itself, may also be viewed as a reflection of several other factors. Most directly reflected are the companies in Hong Kong, Taiwan and elsewhere in close proximity that sometimes establish and directly manage factories in China, and in other cases serve as the link between China and the outside world. Next, there are a variety of brokers located in Hong Kong and elsewhere, largely comprised of Overseas Chinese in overlapping networks of kinship groups that reach to Guangdong and elsewhere throughout the world. Then there are the wholesalers who buy the goods from the brokers, and in turn pass them on to the retailers, and finally the largest group of all, the ultimate consumers (Adams[35]). When these are all taken into account, the enormous export market demand that they represent is nothing less than global.

4. Implications

One of the most fundamental considerations that this subject must address is of course the workers. It is the working conditions and the effects that these conditions have upon the workers that has caught the attention of the world and has generated an extraordinary level of criticism (Ash[36]; National Labour Committee[37], O' Rourke[38]). The simple question that these conditions would seem to pose is how anybody could work under these conditions or why anybody would be willing to work under these conditions. As in all instances of worker exploitation, and even more so the case of extreme worker exploitation, it is reasonable to presume that no one works under these conditions if they have alternatives. Whether they are being drawn from the agricultural North of China, where increasing efficiencies make their labour superfluous, or from state owned enterprises that have gone bankrupt, or are simply redundant employees who have been dismissed from any other kind of enterprise, the alternative to the sweatshop for these workers is unemployment. Relative to the alternatives available to them, the sweatshop factories represent opportunity to those unfortunate enough to have to work there (Kristof and WuDunn[39]).

That these factories represent economic opportunity to so many workers is perhaps best reflected in the city that is at the center of such development in southeastern China, the city of Shenzhen. This is the city in Guangdong Province that can be described as the epicenter of the Special Economic Zone economy. This city, that twenty years ago was a small fishing village, now contains a population estimated at 6 million, with more people trying to enter the city all the time. Since so many of the people living in cities like Shenzhen are there illegally, it is probably impossible to ascertain an accurate count of the population. Entering Shenzhen is like entering a foreign country, it requires a visa–like permit. The city is a gated municipality. It is locked against the untold numbers of poor Chinese people who are anxious to enter and take jobs in its manifold sweat shops. Some newspaper accounts have estimated that there may be as many as 100 million people currently moving through China in search of employment, the floating population (Eckholm[40]). That two-thirds of the population of Shenzhen are probably there illegally, suggests the lengths to which otherwise unemployed individuals will go in search of any kind of work under any conditions.

While there has been considerable criticism of these circumstances from outside China, there has seemingly been relatively little objection or resistance from within. This is a consequence of a confluence of factors. First there is the sheer financial desperation of the otherwise unemployed workers. Second, there are the twin factors of the workers's illegal status in the urban centers where they are working and the government's indifference toward their welfare. But underscoring and cementing these factors may be a pair of related cultural factors. One would be the collective orientation that subordinates the individual to the group, with its corresponding demand for harmonious cooperation (Hofstede[41]; Leung and Kwong[42]). The other would be the degree to which China remains an ideologically socialistic society that reluctantly accommodates free enterprise capitalistic ventures as the available means of economic development (Holt, 1997[43]).

The workers and the shop owners have, in effect, entered into a dirty work agreement, as is often the case in sweatshops, not overtly acknowledging the conditions of work lest their inherent repugnance mandate confrontation and modification. Similar dirty work agreements would seem to characterize the relationship between the Chinese government and the sweatshops and between the sweatshop workers and most of the consumers who buy the goods produced. There is an implicit set of agreements not to confront the reality of the shops so that those who benefit from them do not have to look at the costs or to consider who bears the costs. If these factors are considered in conjunction with the potential number of workers available, it would appear that no significant resistence will emerge from the sweatshop workforce anytime soon.

The factories that these workers fill tend to be small in scale, flexible and anonymous. Since these small-scale manufacturing ventures particularly lend themselves to the production of consumer goods suited for export, they have contributed significantly to China's favorable trade balances. In the Western world today (as well as many other parts of the world) one can buy all manner of manufactured goods made in China, with perhaps the exception of major appliances and automobiles, and the latter are also already being developed through various joint ventures with Western and Japanese corporations that are likely to produce increasing technology transfers (Gan[44]; Thompson[45]). The many small scale manufacturing plants that make these goods offer a number of advantages to China's industrialization. They are flexibly able to engage in a high division of labour, change products quickly, shift production from one site to another and variously serve as contractors and sub-contractors in as complex and shifting a set of relationships as is needed to produce the highest quantity of goods at the lowest possible cost. This is in turn facilitated by the flexibility of the equally complex network of far flung small scale entrepreneurs among the Overseas Chinese, and their commercial networks, who are responsible for much of the distribution of these goods throughout the world (Kwong[46]).

The most obvious beneficiaries of these manufacturing arrangements are the owners of the production facilities, the foreign investors purchasing the goods for resale, and the ultimate consumers of the goods. The benefits, however, extend to a much broader range of beneficiaries in China, owing to the multiplier effects of any productive processes. All those businesses in China that supply materials, build, equip and maintain the productive facilities and ancillary facilities of the sweat shop factories also benefit, as do all those who in turn supply the suppliers, etc., etc. These multiplier effects are further extended when account is taken of the consumer services that those in China benefitting from these businesses further stimulate (Wang and Xu[47]). This combination of economic activities comes to represent a substantial portion of China's urban-industrial economy, and one that is inherently expansive, particularly in comparison to the often less efficient and less profitable state owned enterprises.

In some instances the benefits are indirect and less visible than in others. This is certainly the case for the many people working in the sweatshop factories of Shenzhen and other parts of Guangdong Province who come from the northern parts of China, even as distant as the Northwestern agricultural areas. These are individuals coming from families facing severe economic hardship, often in circumstances where it is impossible to earn a living. For such people the horrible conditions under which they would work in the sweat shops are better than the conditions they leave behind. That people risk their lives climbing over mountains and doing all the things necessary to find their way to these factories, underscores the degree to which the factories represent opportunity to them and their families. Their movement to the industrial areas in the Southeast not only relieves the Northwest agricultural areas of surplus labour, it may also enhance the economy of the Northwest through funds that such workers may be able to send back home.

Another potential source of workers for these factories further reflects the degree to which they will contribute to the overall Chinese economy. Those would be workers displaced from the smaller state-owned factories in China that the government is interested in privatizing, by closing them and dismissing their workers. It will likely also be the case that as the private sector of the economy expands further, it will serve to absorb workers from some of the larger unproductive state-owned industries that the government would also like to shut down if at all possible..

If a parallel is drawn to the experience of industrialization earlier in the western world, then one can anticipate an improvement in working conditions as the industries in China mature and find it desirable and necessary to have a skilled and experienced workforce. Quite likely, the most experienced and skilled workers will be the first to effectively form collective labour organizations and utilize the leverage that their scarcity, their numbers and their solidarity provide. Efforts have already been made to unionize workers in China, but the government has repressed such efforts, preferring the company unions that follow party ideology and that put the interests of the government ahead of the interests of the workers (Eckholm[48]; Xueqin[49]).

Yet another source of modification in the conditions under which factory work is done and the manner in which workers are treated will be the international agreements with other nations that underlie the international organizations that China has been eager to enter into. These would include both ASEAN (Association of South East Asian Nations) and the World Trade Organization (Chirathivat[50]; Woo[51]; Yanfen[52]; Yongtu[53]).

Over the past few years the United States has granted China

Permanent Normal Trade Relations status. This was a status sought by China, reflecting its desire to marry into the economic family of nations. First and foremost among the nations with which China wished to economically marry was the United States. As the largest and richest market in the world, the United States is indispensable to China's development, particularly in relation to the emphasis on export products as a fundamental basis of China's industrialization. The symbiotic and reciprocal relationships that will characterize the accommodations between the two nations, and the other nations that will be involved in these cross cutting relationships, will require mutual adjustments on all sides. The increasingly uniform norms that the other nations have established for workers will put pressure on the Chinese government to bring its industrial facilities into conformity with those norms. This will probably coincide with the pressures already coming from a wide array of countries opposing the sweatshop conditions under which consumer goods are produced in China. Many American college campuses, for example, have become sensitive to the conditions under which their athletic uniforms are produced, refusing to allow the purchase of merchandise from areas where sweat shop conditions prevail.

The adjustments that China will likely make, in the course of these relationships, will not reflect a simple conformity to other nation's norms, so much as a pragmatic set of adjustments necessary to China's own welfare and development. With a relatively young population of 1.2 billion people, 80 percent of whom are still engaged in what is often marginal agriculture, China cannot very patiently await either a demographic transition or an industrial transition in the kind of time frame in which they occurred in the West.

The conditions under which people are working in the sweatshop factories of Southeastern China are clearly horrible at the individual level, yet they serve the larger society well in relation to an accelerated demographic transition and an accelerated industrial transition. The exploitation of the workers generates high levels of profit which, if reinvested, would provide a high level of capitalization for the rapid expansion of industrial facilities. Similarly, the harsh treatment of the female workers, such as locking them in the dormitories at night, discouraging their getting married and firing them if they become pregnant, do serve to accelerate the demographic transition as does an accelerated industrialization. In the broad context of China's development and modernization these individuals may be representative of a whole generation sacrificed in varying ways, and to varying degrees, for the future of the country. Perhaps the most important question that needs to be addressed next is how can the cost of China's economic development be reduced for the factory workers and more evenly distributed throughout the rest of the economy.[54]

Notes and References

1. Chow Kong Wing, Clement and Michael Fung Ka Yiu, "Firm Dynamics and Industrialization in the Chinese Economy in Transition: Implications for Small Business Policy", *Journal of Business Venturing,* 1996, 11, pp. 489-505.
2. Sylvie Demurger, Jeffrey D. Sachs, Wing Thye Woo, Shuming Bao and Gene Chang, "The Relative Contributions of Location and Preferential Policies in China's Regional Development: being in the right place and having the right incentives", *China Economic Review,* 2002, 13, pp. 444-465.
3. Jane Duckett, "Bureaucrats in Business, Chinese Style : The Lessons of Market Reform and State Entrepreneurialism in the People's Republic of China", *World Development,* 2001, 29, pp. 23-37.
4. Allan Gibb and Jun Li, "Organizing for Enterprise in China: What can we Learn From the Chinese Micro, Small, and Medium Enterprise Development Experience", *Futures,* 2003, 35, pp. 403-421.

5. Anita Chan and Robert A, Senser, "China's Troubled Workers", *Foreign Affairs,* 1997, 76, pp. 104-117.
6. Nicholas D. Kristof and Sheryl WuDunn, "Two Cheers for Sweatshops", *The New York Times Magazine,* September 24, 2000, pp. 70-71.
7. Ching Kwan Lee, *Gender and The South China Miracle: Two Worlds of Factory Women,* Berkeley : University of California Press, 1998.
8. Lucy Ash, "Inside China's Sweatshops," http://news.bbc.co.uk/1/hi/worldfrom_our_own_correspondent/2139401.stm, 2002.
9. *National Labor Committee Report on Sweatshop conditions in China,* 2000.
10. Dara O'Rourke, et.al., *Independent University Initiative Final Report,* Cambridge : Massachusetts Institute of Technology, 2000.
11. Karl Marx, "Wage Labour and Capital," in Robert C. Tuckler (ed.), *The Marx-engels Reader,* Second Edition, New York : W.W. Norton & Company, 1978.
12. Yin-Ping Ho, *Hong Kong's* "Trade and Industry: Changing Patterns and Prospects", in Joseph Y.S. Cheng (ed.), *Hong Kong in Transition* Hong Kong : Oxford University Press, 1986.
13. Pui-King Lau, "Economic Relations Between Hong Kong and China", in Joseph Y.S. Cheng (ed.), *Hong Kong in Transition,* Hong Kong: Oxford University Press, 1986.
14. Thomas Chan, Noel Tracy, Wen-Hui Chu, Wen-Hung Chen, *China's Export Miracle : Origins, Results and Prospects,* New York : St. Martin's Press, 1999.
15. Chyau Tuan and Linda Fung-Yee Ng, *Hong Kong's* "Outward Investment and Regional Economic Integration

With Guangdong: Process and Implications", *Journal of Asian Economics,* 1995, 6, pp. 385-405.

16. Justin Yifu Lin, Fang Cai, Zhou Li, *The China Miracle: Development Strategy and Economic Reform,* Hong Kong : The Chinese University Press, 1997.
17. Max Weber, "The Origins of Modern Capitalism (1920)" in Randall Collins (ed.), *Four Sociological Traditions,* New York : Oxford University Press, 1994.
18. Liu Guoguang, "China's Current Economic Development Situation and Prospects", *Journal of Asian Economics,* 1993, 4, pp. 249-254.
19. C.C. Hou, and Jack W. Hou, "Evolution of Economic Institutions and China's Economic Reform", *The Social Science Journal* 2002, 39, pp. 363-379.
20. Seeborg, Michael C., Zhenhu Jin and Yiping Zhu, "The New Rural-Urban Mobility in China : Causes and Implications", *The Journal of Socio-economics,* 2000, 29, pp. 39-56.
21. Jianfa Shen, "Internal Migration and Regional Population Dynamics in China 1978-1990", *Progress in Planning,* 1996, 45, pp. 123-188.
22. Joe C. B. Leung, "Social Welfare Reforms" in Robert Benewick and Paul Wingrove (eds.), *China in The 1990's,* Vancouver : University of British Columbia Press, 1995.
23. Ibid., note 8.
24. Ibid., note 5.
25. Ibid., note 21.
26. M. J. Foster, "South China : are the Rewards Still Worth the Risks?" *Long Range Planning,* 1997, 30, pp. 585-593.
27. Ibid., note 26.
28. Yijiang Wang and Chun Chang, "Economic Transition Under a Semifederalist Government: The Experience of China", *China Economic Review,* 1998, 9, pp. 1-23.

29. Linda Wong and Ngok Kinglun, "Unemployment and Policy Responses in Mainland China", *Issues and Studies : A Journal of Chinese Studies and International Affairs*, 1997, 33, pp. 43-63.

30. Ibid., note 29.

31. Ibid., note 20.

32. Harry Harding, *China's Second Revolution: Reform After Mao*, Washington : Brookings Institution, 1987.

33. Chung Chen, Lawrence Chang and Yimin Zhang, "The Role of Foreign Direct Investment in China's Post-1978 Economic Development", *World Development*, 1995, 23, pp. 691-703.

34. K.C. Fung, Hitomi Iizaka and Stephen Parker, "Determinants of U.S. and Japanese Direct Investment in China", *Jouirnal of Comparative Economics*, 2002, 30, pp. 567-578.

35. Ronald J. Adams, "Retail profitability and sweatshops: a global dilemma", *Journal of Retailing and Consumer Services"*, 2002, 9, pp.147-153.

38. Ibid., note 8.

37. Ibid., note 9.

38. Ibid., note 10.

39. Ibid., note 6.

40. Erik Eckholm, "Silk Workers in Standoff With Beijing Over Union", *The New York Times*, December 15, 2000, p. 6.; "Tide of China's Migrants : Flowing to Boom or Bust?", *The New York Times*, July 29, 2003, A1.

41. Hofstede, Geert, *Culture's Consequences: International Differences In Work-related Values*, Newbury Park (CA): Sage Publishing, 1980.

42. Kwok Leung and Jessica Y.Y. Kwong, "Human Resource

Management Practices in International Joint Ventures in Mainland China: a Justice Analysis", *Human Resource Management Review,* 2003, 13, pp. 85-105.

43. David H. Holt, "A Comparative Study of Values Among Chinese and U.S. Entrepreneurs: Pragmatic Convergence Between Contrasting Cultures", *Journal of Business Venturing,* 1997, 12, pp. 483-505.

44. Lin Gan, "Globalization of the Automobile Industry in China: Dynamics and Barriers in Greening of the Road Transportation", *Energy Policy,* 2003, 31, pp. 537-551.

45. Edmund R. Thompson, "Clustering of Foreign Direct Investment and Enhanced Technology Transfer: Evidence from Hong Kong Garment Firms in China", *World Development,* 2002, 30, pp. 873-889.

46. Peter Kwong, "The Chinese Diaspora", *World Business,* May/June, 1996, pp. 26-31.

47. James Jixian Wang and Jiang Xu, "An Unplanned Commercial District in a Fast-Growing City: A Case Study of Shenzhen, China", *Journal of Retailing and Consumer Services,* 2002, 9, pp. 317-326.

48. Ibid., note 40.

49. Jiang Xueqin, "Fighting to Organize", *Far Eastern Economic Review,* 6 September 2001, p. 72.

50. Suthiphand Chirathivat, "ASEAN-China Free Trade Area: Background, Implications and Future Development", *Journal of Asian Economics,* 2002, 13, pp. 671-686.

51. Wing Thye Woo, "Recent claims of China's economic exceptionalism: Reflections inspired by WTO accession", *China Economic Review,* 2001, 12, pp. 107-136.

52. Liang Yanfen, "The Impact on China's Enterprises of Joining WTO", *The Chinese Economy,* 2000, 33, pp. 33-41.

53. Long Yongtu, "On the Question of Our Joining the World

Trade Organization", *The Chinese Economy*, 2000, 33, pp. 5-52.

54. An earlier version of this paper was presented at the American Sociological Association Annual Meeting in Anaheim California on August 19, 2001.

****

6

Threshold Effects of Globalization on Poverty, Unemployment, Youth and Religion in India

Sanman Jain N*, Mairaj Salim**, and Nishi Verma**

1. Introduction

Globalization is defined by different people in different ways. It is a complex phenomenon. It is a process by which the world becomes a "global village." Globalization affects different aspects of any country—economic, political, social, and religious.

"Globalization —What is it all about?" It deals with a definition for globalization. According to Kurian, "It is a concept used as a short form to convey a wide variety of processes possibilities, and positions. It is, therefore, capable of different kinds of interpretations. Hence to say anything meaningful about globalization, including how to respond to it, there is need to know as clearly as possible what it is all about". It talks about the marvelous technological innovations such as e-mail and flights that convert this earth and its people into a "global village." But this globe has been integrated by capitalist practices and ideology and has largely removed ideological polarization. So his conclusion is that it is a concept, the meaning

* Sr. Faculty in Management, NICE Management College, Modipuram, Meerut (India).

** Sr. Faculty in Management, NICE Management College, Modipuram, Meerut (India).

** Lecturer in Management, NICE Management College, Roorkee Road, Meerut (India).

and implications of which cannot be taken for granted and that one cannot define one's response to it until the concept is adequately specified. He is an economist, and he says that the economic and political triumph of private capital and its presence throughout the world is the main component of what has come to be celebrated as "globalization."[1.]

2. What Globalization is in terms of the People of India?

Globalization is not a remote experience or removed from the lives of the ordinary people of India. If foreign capital brings in new technology, it may either increase employment, or more likely reduce employment. New capital that comes in is likely to go into the production of goods that cater to the needs of those who have high purchasing power because the profits are likely to be higher in such spheres. This may create an impression that there is growth and prosperity. But the needs of the bulk of the population may tend to be neglected. There will be no sense of accountability to Indian people in this process. The local manufacturers and workers may be replaced. This is happening to the handloom weavers in different parts of India. It also mentions that globalization usually benefits people who can play the game, but the chances are that the many who are resource less, uneducated, and making a living through traditional production activities, will come under various kinds of pressures. So he suggests that we need to educate people about the nature and implications of globalization and its different facilities, and train in skills for young people according to the new trends.

In New Horizons, "Contemporary India and Popular Culture," speaks about India's changes very well: Modern India has its stark contrasts and its own share of contradictions. It is the largest democracy alive. It is emerging with its liberalization and market reforms, as one of the dynamic major Asian economies. It is a world leader in several areas – its indigenous-built communications satellites have been successfully launched, it has the best computer software in the world, its telecommunications technology has successfully reached the remotest rural areas, and it has a strong army. Yet it is one of the poorest countries in the world, with a population expected to touch world's highest and a high illiteracy rate[2].

But at the same time, we can say that India has embraced a market economy, and as a result it has lead to unequal distribution of income and wealth which in turn leads to unequal distribution of power and hence to the exploitation of those with economic power over those who lack sufficient economic power. This has led to the over-exploitation of natural resources of India, damages to the environment, pollution, and other such evils.

3. Globalization and Poverty

The concept of globalization and poverty remain the objects of intense debate, in particular over the definitions and indicators of globalization: for example, integration in the commodity, labour and capital markets[3], 'freedom and ability of individuals and firms to initiate voluntary economic transactions with residents of other countries', and 'greater mobility of capital and labour'[4]. Globalization encompasses heterogeneous elements: facts (flows, such as trade, capital, labour, migration, information, and market integration) and policies (reduction of barriers on trade, financial flows and migration, liberalisation). Depending on the aspects of globalization considered, the functions of institutions differ: providing credibility to government's domestic commitments and policies, enforcing property rights for foreign investment, and reducing information costs and allowing the pooling of risks for small-scale farmers.

4. Globalization and its Effect on Youth in India

Several times we discuss about how youth in India are affected by globalization of media, travels, fashions, and economic changes. Youth in India may be 50 percent to 60 percent of the population of India. India has embarked on economic, social, and political changes. Our productivity has increased a lot, but we are not keeping it up with our population growth. The economic growth has helped our upper and middle class grow, but the poor are still very poor, and there is a large group of people in this category.

Youth, in increasingly larger numbers, have a high level of unemployment particularly in the urban centers. Urban poverty is growing faster, and the causes are the increased rural-urban migration, mismanagement of scarce available resources, corruption, untapped and wasted population, severe natural calamities, civil and ethnic conflict leading to acts of violence, and denial of fundamental rights of humanity in different states. Among the Scheduled Castes and Dalits, our youth are still struggling to come up. There are quotas in educational institutions and in employment, but even to reach that level, the environment prohibits them. In the highly competitive private sector Dalits cannot compete on an equal footing due to lack of opportunity, skilled training, and education. Globalization adversely affects Dalits in many ways[5].

5. Globalization and its Impact on Religion(s)

Globalization has affected our religious situation very much. We have had strong ethnicity in India from the very beginning. We had fights between Hindus and Muslims from the beginning of our Independence. Gandhi (the father of nation) was murdered by a fanatic fellow Hindu for urging fair treatment of Muslims. Gandhi became a martyr because he held up the ideal of a secular India in which all faiths would be treated equally. For all its newly found modernism, India remains steeped in religion. "The overwhelming majority of its millions of population are Hindus, [but it is] also home to over millions of Muslims, Christians, Sikhs, Buddhists, Jains, and countless adherents of other faiths.

In the villages people live peacefully. But in the cities the politicians use young people for their vested interests and thus sacrifice communal peace. By nature Indian people are religious and the majority of people have practiced a spirit of tolerance. This has been destroyed by manipulative politicians for narrow ends.

Globalization has caused social unrest and communalism in India: "...as a result of globalization the individual is atomized through fierce competition for survival .... The general atmosphere of speculation leads to a gambler's mentality which is compounded by the prevalence of insecurity and impermanence. The indirect, invisible and covert nature of the oppressive forces leads to a non-focused anger and anxiety....Globalization has thus been contemporaneous with an increase in the assertion of ethnic-religious-linguistic subnationalities"[6]. Thus globalization has contributed to the growth of communalism in India.

If we look at this issue of ethnicity, we will come to the same conclusion. Myers says, "First, whatever is coming probably will contain an alternative to the free market as we know it today .... Second, globalism will not be the sole defining reality, as some suggest. Globalism does not provide a satisfactory home for the individual human being. The market may be global, communication may be global, the technology may be global, but I never will be. Human beings need a place, a story, a set of relationships. This is why ethnicity and religion are emerging as such powerful counter-forces to globalism today"[7].

6. Globalization and its Impact on Indian Society

Indian society is drastically changing as a result of globalization. "Cultural imperialism has two major goals—one economic and the other political—to capture markets for its cultural commodities and to establish hegemony by shaping popular consciousness .... Cultural domination is an integral dimension of any sustained system of global exploitation."[8] There is a systematic cultural penetration and domination of the cultural life of the popular class by the ruling class of the West in order to reorder the values, behavior, institutions, and identity of the oppressed people to conform with the interests of the imperial class.

Indians traditionally have followed the joint family system. Contemporary times have seen changes in these family institutions, and the nuclear family system is increasing to become the norm. So far, the concept of single parenthood hasn't caught on in the Indian culture. Divorce rates are increasing. Urbanization has brought a lot of changes in Indian culture. Many marriages are breaking up for many reasons, such as modern life-styles, professional ambitions, and unrealistic expectations. Commitment for marriage is disappearing as a result of modernization in India now[9].

In cities young people are starting to choose their own partners. Arranged marriages, however, still exist. The upper class and middle class people of India and the urban Indians have changed a lot of their cultural values as a result of the impact of TV and industrialization. Consumerism has permeated and changed the fabric of contemporary Indian society.

Fashions are coming to India. Traditional Indian dress is changing, especially with urban youth. All these things have eroded the traditional beliefs and practices of the Indian people. Ahimsa (non-violence) and aparigraha (non-attachment) was our Indian heritage and culture. Some of the changes are good. Women have raised their voices and have changed some cultural expectations. But many major changes are not helpful to the community.

7. Conclusions: Resultant Issues of Globalization in India

In a large population of India the majority is young population. India's population is growing at faster rate and by the year 2010, we may reach 1.5 billion. "By 2030, 60 percent of the world's population will live in Asia where India and China are the major players. The huge bulk of the population of India is living in the cities. There are many pressing problems our country is facing. Now deal with a few of them here:

7.1 Poverty and Unemployment

Poverty in this era of globalization has assumed new dimensions. Globalization and marginalization go hand in hand. What prospects are there for the millions of poor peasants, rural labourers, urban unemployed, slum-dwellers, millions of refugees, millions of street children, and the millions displaced by 'the development' projects.

Health care also was cut. The sharpest cuts occurred in preventive disease control programs such as those for malaria, tuberculosis, and leprosy. The poor suffered most. The cut-down of rations has led to an increase in the number of persons below the poverty line. Agricultural as well as industrial unemployment increased especially in rural areas. Prices of major commodities increased. Impoverishment exacerbates gender inequality within each household.

Land has been taken away from the poor, and they have been displaced from their traditional employment without being provided any alternative. Pollution of drinking water is another problem. Due to uncontrolled industrialization, globalization intensifies the problem of safe drinking water. The mechanization of agriculture through use of tractors and harvesters displaces labour. So the workers are forced to sell their labour power cheaply. Migrant labour is also increasingly used. Unemployed Adivasis, Dalits, and OBCs are given small advances during lean periods and are then compelled to work as seasonal migrants at very low wages. Bonded labourers are the result of globalization. Most of these are young people.

Computerization has helped the middle class youth in India get more jobs in that field. Many people are migrating to other countries where job opportunities are better. India has been one of the leading countries for supplied programmers to many other countries for computer Y2K problems. India has computerized every field or work to be a global competitor. IBM, Hewlett Packard, and Compaq have established extensive networks in India. Computers have flooded the market and prices have dropped drastically in recent months. Internet and e-mail facilities are easily accessible in all work places. Globalisation and Liberalization has helped in reducing unemployment for middle class and upper class young people to some extent, but not enough.

7.2 Lack of Technical and Skilled Training

India has advanced to provide technical training in the field of computer, engineering, and so on. But we need a lot more programmes and inputs in such areas to meet our employment needs. Our educational system is more degree oriented and most of those degrees do not include training in skills for jobs. So even after earning a degree, the students often do not get jobs. Our educational system should change according to the needs created by globalization.

7.3 The Impact of Global Media on Youth

The youth constitute the most vulnerable group to the influence of the media. Three characteristics of youth—a search for identity, the craving for freedom, and the push and pull of sexuality—make them very exploitable. The teenagers are the most global market of all. Studies reveal the startling fact that in all major cities of the world teenagers and young adults between 20 and 25 have the same tastes.

A study of urban youth in India revealed that youth viewers make up approximately 31%. From the media young people get the inspiration for their life-styles, patterns of behaviour, dress codes, and jargon. Rural India is not too far behind. TV and film culture has invaded even our village youth. Youth are the target of media campaigns. Media uses youth more than any other group.

According to some studies and conferences the effect of the media on India; media's impact is very high on the cultural values of youth who are already in a stage of identity crisis where they reject adult authority. So when extra push and freedom is given to them, they misuse the freedom. In the urban areas without proper guidance, youth may reject the authority of elders and make serious mistakes in their lives.

Face of India is changing. Changes are occurring in our culture, social institutions, and interpersonal relationships as well. The market-oriented, media-driven western influence has affected India in no small measure. With the advent of satellite connections, almost all the international news, commercials, soap operas, and games can be seen. If America has its Hollywood, India has the Bombay-based Bollywood. It has its fair share of sex, crime, and violence. It sets the fashions, attitudes, and life style of people today, especial of the youth. Western songs and rhythms have influenced Indian films and changed our taste of music, especially for our youth. Even in Hindi films words in English are used side by side with Hindi.

Consumerism has permeated and changed the fabric of contemporary Indian society. Buying the latest cars, TVs, electronic gadgets, and trendy clothes has become quite popular. Levi and Lee jeans and T-shirts, ladies' dresses, from midis to maxis, and skirts have almost replaced the traditional Indian sari. TV commercials and advertisements have influenced the buying habits of our youth. When the poor cannot respond to these ads, they get frustrated, and as a result crime increases.

7.4 Family Values: Radical Changes

Earlier we dealt briefly about the changes which are occurring in Indian culture as a whole. Here we want to look at how this is affecting our youth in India. Youth between the ages of 13 and 23 are already undergoing very upsetting changes at various depths of their personalities—physically, intellectually, emotionally, and spiritually. This transition means surrendering the ownership by parents and entering into one's self-possession—a period of searching, questioning, doubting, and fraught with its successes as well as failures. Exploration, curiosity, and adventure can sometimes cross socially acceptable limits." Peer group pressure is very high, and young people need recognition from peers. So they get into all sorts of bad habits like drugs, alcohol, and smoking. In cities parents give a lot more freedom now than before; so youth get into a lot more trouble.

The young mind is fertile for ideologies and experimentation. Give a cause and youth will die for it. The Mandal immolations and Ayodha demolition are vivid examples of the fanatical potential of misdirected youthful idealism. Media is partly to blame for the inconsistency of young people. Crazy fashions promoted by the world of business keep challenging youth to be outrageously daring and different.

7.5 Social Upheavals: Crime and Violence

As previously mentioned, religious violence has increased in India. Recently newspapers and TV programs have shown a lot more crimes than before. Has globalization anything to do with this? Yes. It has brought insecurity and restlessness to young people, and when they have no jobs and secure future, they become agitated and crime-oriented. Parental authority also has been weakened, causing a lack of control and guidance. Because of the increased consumerism, the breakdown of family, the unbearable pressure of competition, and the impact of the media, violence is coming out of the air, as it were, from the movies and cable TV[10]. In case both are parents are working they may have no time for their children. The joint family system has weakened; consequently there are no relatives or grandparents to take care of the children. Many women in India are working for survival. All these changes have affected young people.

7.6 Sex and Moral Decay

Already insecure with their identity, young people experience greater confusion in the area of sex. Parents and elders are reticent and hesitate to talk about it. Unfortunately, this is often the first education youth receive in sexual matters. Infatuation is called love. Sex and love are projected as interchangeable. In urban societies, there is comparatively less supervision of young people, and this gives them freedom to experiment with sex much earlier. The United Nations Population Fund released a paper based on eight independent studies conducted across India. It indicated that 1 out of 10 boys below 16 years of age has had sexual experiences. The prevalence of premarital sex was found to be higher in urban areas than in rural areas. Teenage pregnancies are reaching an all-time high in India.

They find information about sex on TV talk shows and on soaps. Parents are not taking time to educate their children about sex. Abstinence was the Indian culture, but globalization has definitely changed it. New Age parenting is about dumping conservative values and wearing a more liberal, uninhibited face. In urban areas, girls are allowed out more easily. Dating isn't altogether taboo and there is much less adult supervision. All this has brought down the moral and ethical decay of the values of young people in India.

7.7 Young Women's Issues: Prostitution, Aids, Abortion, Abuse

Through our internet search we found many articles on the subject of globalization and its effect on women. Globalization has attributed to displacement, commodification, and modern-day slavery of women in Asia. Those that are greatly affected are industries of predominantly women who work in jobs dealing with textiles and clothing, electronics, food, and other assembly type industries. The worsening poverty in Third World countries; has led to thousands of women going to other countries to find better opportunities. Migration policies by sending governments have encouraged the trafficking in women, as trading in women's bodies has become a very lucrative industry at a very limited investment. Modern-day slavery of women brought about by globalization. It is clearly seen in women's through prostitution.

Prostitution is prevalent in the big cities in India as well. The red-light districts of Mumbai are very well known, and tourism has helped in increasing this trade. With regard to AIDS in India, there are HIV positives and a lot more untested people with AIDS in India. Most of these spreading is happening through heterosexual activities. Women are the main victims in this situation. Women and men need to be educated on prevention and care of AIDS.

Abuse of women was prevalent in India before globalization. But globalization has caused the increase of it because of the stress and strain of the community and the changes in the traditional life style. In the joint family system there were social control systems which helped women in these issues. But in the individualistic life styles now, women suffer more abuse. Indian women have been suffering under many traditional evils, such as dowry, low image of women, and inequality.

7.8 What does this have to do with Globalization?

Globalization has increased the greed of people for more goods, and as a result, more dowry is demanded for young women. This has made it worse for young women and their parents to meet the dowry demands of a new TV, car, and other articles of luxury. The government has passed some laws against these bad traditions, but have not been able to remove them. More dowry is demanded now than previously. Women's organizations are working hard to change these evils in our society, but we have a long way to go. Some women's organizations are trying to educate women about the laws which are already there, as many women are not yet aware of them.

7.9 Migration: From Rural to Urban and from India to Other Countries

We are having more people living in our cities than in rural areas. This is the result of urbanization. This phenomena is both good and bad. But it is an irreversible phenomena. Many educated Indians are going abroad in search of jobs. There are thousands of doctors in the U.S.A. from India. There are many engineers, professors, teachers, computer specialists, and other business people in the U.S.A. and in other countries. Many Indians are working in other Asian countries and Arabian countries as well. Economically Indian people do very well. These people do help their relatives in India. So this is helping India in some ways. But the brain drain is very high. Many of these people are trained in India and the Indian government has spent large amounts of money on them (our education is subsidized by the government). So other countries benefit from Indian human resources.

Notes and References

1. Kurian C.T., "Globalisation-What is it about?" in *Integral Liberation*, Vol. I, No. 3 Sept., Allied Publisher, New Delhi, 1997, pp. 135-136.
2. Samuel, Manohar, "Contemporary India and Popular Culture" in *New Horizons United Board for Christian Higher Education in Asia,* 65:3, Summer, 1998, pp. 1-12
3. Taylor and Willimson, *Definitions*, Bordo Publishing House, New York, 2003.
4. World Bank, *Definitions and Quotes*, Milanovic Report, 2003.
5. *India Today* articles "Crime Time" (May 11, 1998, pp. 56-57, August 1, 1998, p. 55).
6. Kaarda, John Desrecher and Allan M. Pannal, Editors, *Complementary Insights on Globalization*, Sage Publications, Newbury Park, 1993, pp. 144-145
7. Myers,Bryant, "What Is Going On?" Subtitle "After

Modernity, What?" *MARC News Letter*, No. 98-4, 1998, pp. 5

8. Kaarda, John Desrecher and Allan M. Pannal, Editors, "Complementary Insights on Globalization" in *Integral Liberation*, 1:3, September 3, Sage Publications, Newbury Park, 1997, pp. 176-150,161
9. Sheela Raval, "Till Whims Do Us Part," under section called 'Marriages' in *India Today*, Aug. 1, 1998, pp.60-61
10. Madhu Jain, *India Today* in a section called "Society and Trends," there was an article called: "Growing Up in Anger: Children are increasingly turning aggressive as result of family breakdown and the impact of media" p. 66.

****

7

Globalization, Multinationals and the Indian Private Sector

*Susheel Kumar**
*Manju Lata***

The term 'Globalization' is coming up today as a catchword. Its change is not confined to economics and politics alone. Broadly speaking, the term 'globalization' means integration of economics and societies through cross country flows of information, ideas, technologies, goods, services, capital, finance and people. The essence of globalization is connectivity. In fact, some people fear cultural and social integration even more then economic integration.

However, the term globalization is used here in the limited sense of economic integration, which can happen through the three channels of:

(a) Trade in goods and services,

(b) Movement of capitals and

(c) Flow of Finance.

Besides, there is also a channel through movement of people.

During the first three decades of planned industrialization in India (1950s to the mid-1970s), the role in guiding outcomes both in the labour market as well as within the organized labour movement.

* Department of Geography, C.C.S. University, Meerut (U.P.), India
** Department of Sociology, R.G. College, Meerut (U.P.), India

1. A Historical Process

In common parlance 'Globalization' is supposed to be a 'new found phenomenon' However, this is far from reality. In fact, globalization is as old as history itself, starting with the large migration of people across the great landmasses. During the pre world war period of 1870 to 1914, there was rapid integration of the economics in terms of trade flows, movement of capital and migration of people. The inter-war period witnessed the creation of various barriers to restrict free movement of goods and services. Although after 1945 there was a drive to increased integration, studies point out that trade and capital markets are no more globalized today than they were at the end of the 19th century. However, there are more concerns about globalization now than ever before because of the nature and speed of transformation. What is striking in the current episode is not only the rapid pace but also the enormous impact of globalization on various aspects of society.

2. Multinationals

The post-war period witnessed the emergence of a hitherto unknown corporate entity–multinationals corporations—the gigantic business enterprises undertaking direct foreign investments through their establishment spread over a large number of countries. They sprawled across national boundaries and the general markets of national jurisdiction under a single focus of control. The fruits of science in the form of instant communication, quick transport, sophisticated computers and modern managerial techniques have been helping them in reshuffling costs, prices and availabilities of large untapped sellers markets and cheap labour force in developing.

Till 1970s, multinationals were geographically confined to the free enterprise economics. During the past three decades, however, countries with planned economics or the so-called "people's democracies" have also entered in to deals with the MNCs to set up their countries on a license basis. In most of the developing countries, one may find dozens of MNCs, operating under varying conditions like 100 percent owned subsidiaries, collaboration governments with equity participation in the companies. The fast-eroding base of communism and socialism seems to have provided the multinationals with fresh impetus for widening their areas of operation.

Indian Perspective: As far as India is concerned, a host of multinationals have been in operation for about four decades in diverse fields such as; tobacco, pharmaceuticals, toiletries, beverages manufacturing industries etc. World Investment Report, UNCTAD, 2000 listed over 100 largest multinationals of the world; nearly half of them are operating in India.

A dispassionate appraisal of the role of multinationals in our country may lead one to conclude that they have contributed to our development efforts in these distinct ways:

(1) First they have promoted new technology through local research by utilizing indigenous raw materials instead of imports.

(2) Globalization in its present form though spurred by far reaching technological changes is not a pure technological phenomenon. It has many dimensions including ideological.

(3) Finally, the cadre of professional managers they have groomed is acknowledged to be one of the best in the world.

Besides, they have contributed substantially in mobilizing much needed finance for the multidimensional growth of the Indian economy.

3. Globalization and After

All these factors seem to have facilitated the entry, existence and expansion of multinational corporations in India. Besides, the current wave of globalization and liberalization also played a distinct role in playing way for the multinationals in diverse areas of the Indian economy "In the wake of recent developments in the global business system in favour of market—driven economy, increasing economic interdependence and globalization of markets and emergence of the World Trade Organization, the Government of India resorted to cataclysmic policy reforms, opening the floodgates of the domestic market to the multinationals with the principal objective of increasing competitiveness in Indian business and accelerating the pace of economic development."

Table : Employee Strength of MNCs Operating in Developed Market in India

Vendor	2001-2002	2002-03	2003-04	2004-05	Global
Cap Gemini E & Y	700	1,200	7,000	NA	80,000
CSC	250	800	1,500	2,700	50,000
Deloitte Touche	600	1000	2,000	3,500	15,000
EDS	700	1100	2,000	3,000	1,38,000
IBM G.S	4300	6500	8,200	10,000	1,250,000
Cognizant	2712	6500	8,500	11,500	–
Logica CMG	NA	300	500	700	21,000

Source—Business World, 1st Sept., 2003.

4. Long-term Strategy

The long term strategy for combating the multi dimensional challenges of the multinationals has to be crafted within the parameters of corporate purposes and mission and long term objectives. In the changed economic milieu of India and abroad, Indian firms will have to draw up their futuristic vision by way of redefining their corporate purpose and mission and resting their attainable objectives. Through purpose and mission, a firm has to visualize what business it desires to engage in and where the primary emphasis has to be placed. A firm to survive and grow must customaries its purpose so that its entire efforts are focused in customaries satisfaction in terms of low price, high quality and service. The managers and the workers who will be called upon to translate it into reality must share the new vision. Within the Framework of overall corporate purpose and mission, the firm has to craft out long term achievable objectives especially in critical areas. However, in the changed environment the immediate goal of a firm has to be survival for which emphasis will have to be placed a maximizing market share rather than an maximizing profit. The ultimate objective of the firm should be to achieve international competitiveness.

Indian corporate may have a competitive edge over the multinationals in respect of their access to natural resources and cheep labour. This coupled with high domestic as well as foreign demand, present tremendous opportunities to Indian firms in agro-based industries, steel, paper, cement, fertilizers, teretiles, leather, power generation etc. It is these areas, which are receiving increasing attention of the multinationals. It must, however, be noted that in a globalized economy that is competing with technology and reduced resources and labour intensity one cannot sustain competitive advantage that way in the long run. This can be achieved through technological excellence better productivity and product differentiation.

Changes in policy environment in the third world countries are offering tremendous opportunities to Indian firms primarily because of the fact that our level of technology suits their, needs for instance, South Africa and Asian countries are very attractive markets for vehicles and goods carriers, footwear's and dyestuffs. Israel is forgetting India as a market for its agro-technology, health care and environment technology. And for India, Israel is a good base to sell garments and textiles.

By matching care competency and other capabilities, the corporate after natives and evaluate each of them and choose the one that accomplishes the corporate objective of combating threads from multinationals at home and emerging as major player in the own right in global markets.

Indian corporate will, therefore, have to adopt consolidation strategy followed by growth strategy and concentrate in the beginning only in those product market areas where they would confine themselves to certain potential areas such as cement, steel, paper, machine—tools, electrical and electronics, automobiles power generation, consumer durables and consumer non-durables.

To sum up, if Indian companies invest more in product quality and customer service they would certainly succeed in taking any challenge, big or small. To be able to do so, however Indian industry must become more quality conscious invest in human capital and R and D and encourage professional management to do a professional job.

India has been home to enterprizing people for centuries. Indians abroad, the great Indian Diaspora, have demonstrated to the world that its entrepreneurial and professional skills are the best. With more investment at home on our people, on their education, skills and health, on an improved and globally, competitive infrastructure sector and the willingness to take on the World, Indian business can hopefully look forward to one era of rejuvenation, growth and diversifications in the new millennium.

Notes and References

1. I. J. Ahluwalia *Productivity and Growth in Indian Manufacturing Centre for Policy Research,* New Delhi (Mimeo), 1991.

2. Das Jackson "Wage Policy and Industrial Relations in India" *in Economic Journal,* Vol. 82, March 1972, p. 93.

3. V. Joshi and M. D. Little, *India: Macro Economics and Political Economy,* 1969-91, The World Bank, 1994.

4. T. S. Papola "Employment Growth and Social Protection of Labour in India" in *Indian Journal of Industrial Relations,* Vol. 30, 1994.

5. G. A. Ramaswamy, *Power and Justice*, Oxford University Press, New Delhi, 1984.

6. V. D. Kennedy, *Linins, Employers and Government*, Manaktales, Mumbai, 1966.

****

8

Social Change by Education among Scheduled Castes in the Era of Globalization

*Hemlata Sharma**
*Geeta Chaudhary**
*Ravinder Saini**

1. Introduction

The world has become a global village in modern era. Globalization refers to mutual interdependence of the countries of the world particularly their economic interdependence and freedom to integrate with one another through trade, investments and capital flows. Globalization has economic, political, social, cultural and several other dimensions. The process of globalization in India is expected to bring changes in the spheres of economic, culture, education and other aspects of life. Education occupies an important place in modern human lives, and more so, in cases of groups, which are historically deprived and marginalized in Indian society, namely Scheduled Castes and Scheduled Tribes its role is important. It becomes more important in the era of globalization.

The social change occurring due to education in this era of globalization is important and need the attention of the social science scholars.

M.S.A. Rao[1] considers that education is a major determinant that is a contributing factor, in socialization of the younger generation, which influences the values, attitudes and norms

* Research Scholars, Department of Sociology, C.C.S. University, Meerut (U.P.), India.

of behaviour accepted in the society to which they belong as by passing on specific forms of knowledge, skills or occupational techniques. N.J. Usha Rao[2] observes that education is a relevant component of development index. Education not only improves the skills of people leading to increase in the level of productivity, it plays a major role in social change. Education, particularly technical and vocational education, helps the people in securing employment and increasing their levels of income, consumption and living standards and socio-economic status of people.

Many social scientists beginning from the founders of sociology like Emile Durkheim consider that education is major factor and causes social change. Indian sociologists like S. Chitnis[3], N.K. Singhi[4], S. Patwardhan[5], N. J. Usha Rao[6], M. L. Jha[7], P. N. Pandey[8], C. Parvathamma[9] have highlighted that the Scheduled Castes population achieving education and education plays an important role in getting higher status and thus social change. Still all these studies leave scope for further studies on education among Scheduled Castes and Consequential Social Change. Therefore, to broaden the base of generalization on this issue further and continuous studies are required.

The present paper aims at finding out the Social Change occurring as a consequence of education among Scheduled Castes in this era of globalization. This study highlights two specific issues in the context of Scheduled Castes, namely, (1) Educational change among Scheduled Castes in the era of globalization (2) Consequential change of education in their social life patterns, political and economic aspects.

The objectives have been studied in a Mohalla, Shergarhi, situated in I block of Shastri Nagar, of Meerut city in Western Uttar Pradesh. 100 respondents through purposive sampling method have selected for the study, quasi participate observation and interview method have been used as main technique of data collection.

2. Theoretical Perspective

A. Giddens[10] states that the globalization is a consequence of modernity and has in fact complemented a general perspective that one finds widely in the so called Third World and other non-western region of the globe, as well as in political circles in the West. This perspective centres on the proclamation that the West enjoys what is often called hegemonic position in the world as a whole. In a certain sense, then it is in the interests of those who maintain that they are representing subaltern or oppressed groups to cast the west as very dominant and thus to conceive of globalization as a form of westernization or as imperialism or colonialism in a new guise. In this perspective, many non-western societies are regarded as victims without agency and 'globalization' becomes simply a pejorative symbol of all things that are allegedly contaminating or disrupting these societies.

S. Paswan and P. Jaideva[11] take that education not only improves the skills of people leading to increase in the level of productivity but also plays a major role in social change. Education, particularly technical and vocational education, helps the people in securing employment and increasing their levels of income, consumption and living standards and social economic status of people. Hence, special attention was paid for the educational development of Dalits by allocating 50 percent of Dalits, for their education.

N.K. Singhi[12], observes that education is an important indicator of the social status. Education influences the process of social change amongst Scheduled Castes and Scheduled Tribes people. Social change in the context of Scheduled Castes and Scheduled Tribes categories imply creating conditions through such appropriate means whereby these people do not continue to remain deprived due to their status-ascription nor due to any institutionalized disabilities.

S. Patwardhan[13] considers that education as a status symbol, and higher education is not only a status symbol but also an effective means to upper mobility. The changes are occurring among the Harijans, social change and social mobility as two theoretical and integral aspects. Change is studies with specific reference to mobility.

M. L. Jha[14] considers that educational development and expansion among the Scheduled Castes will surely ~~help~~ change their traditional occupation and low levels of living standard.

C. Parvathamma[15] asserts that education is one of the important variables with the help of which social change could be achieved. The government followed the policy of protective discrimination for the welfare of Scheduled Castes and Scheduled Tribes. In the field of education certain number of seats or percentage of seats are reserved on the basis of Scheduled Castes/Scheduled Tribes population. Reservation in job opportunities is extended to Scheduled Castes/Scheduled Tribes.

3. Educational Change

In the first part of the study we have analyzed the educational change among Scheduled Castes in the era of globalization in following aspects-educational change from past to present generation, equality of educational opportunity among males and females, sex ratio of Scheduled Castes at various levels of education.

The Education is most important factor to help people for a better way of life style and to use opportunities in wider society. Education acts as cause and determination of social change. Education can be cause of social change and can be effected by social change.

Table—1 : Educational Changes between two generations of Scheduled Caste Respondents

Education	Past Generation	Present Generation	Change
Illiterate	80	08	-72
Primary	15	09	-06
Jr. High School	05	03	-02
High School	00	15	+15
Intermediate	00	15	+15
Graduate	00	24	+24
Post Graduate	00	21	+21
B.A./M.A.+ Prof. Course	00	05	+05
Total	**100**	**100**	

The above table shows that the (80percent) of the respondents of previous generation were illiterate whereas there are (8 percent) of the respondents are illiterate in present generation. At the primary level of education the number has decreased, 15 percent of the respondents of previous generation and 9 percent of the respondents in the present generation. In Jr. High School 8 percent in the previous generation and 3 percent in the present generation. No one educated above Jr. High School in previous generation and 15 percent of the respondents are in High School and 15 percent of the respondents in Intermediate. 24 percent respondents are in graduation, 21% are in the post graduation. 9 percent of the respondents are in the graduation post-graduation with professional course in the present generation.

Thus, the facts show that the past-generation largest segments 80 percent respondents were illiterate but in the present generation lowest 8 percent of the respondents are illiterate in the present generation largest 50 percent of the respondents are high educated. Thus, the education level has increased day by day.

3.1 Equality of Education

Equal right of male-female education is an important variable of social change.

Table-2: Scheduled Castes Respondents fell equality of Male-Female education

Education	Equal	Somewhat	No Change	No. of Respondents
Less	07	05	05	17
Moderate	24	09	00	33
High	47	03	00	50
Total	**78**	**17**	**05**	**100**

Thus the facts shows that largest segment 78 percent of the respondents fell equal opportunity to male-female education and the lowest 05 percent of the respondents feel no equality in male-female education in their families. In the present time people give equal opportunities to male-female education.

3·2 Sex-ratio in Education

In the changing social environment sex-ratio in education also change, which is responsible further social change.

Table—3 : Sex-ratio of Scheduled Caste Respondents in Education

Education	Male	Female	No. of Respondents
Less	07	10	17
Moderate	21	12	33
High	17	28	50
Total	**45**	**55**	**100**

The fact shows that 45 percent of the respondents are male, among them 17 percent are highly educated, 21 percent are moderate educated, 07 percent are less educated, 55 percent of the respondents are females, among them 28% are highly educated, 12 percent are moderate educated, 10% are less educated.

4. Change in Social Life Patterns

In the second part of the study we have analyse the change is social life patterns among scheduled caste in the area of globalization in following aspects—social life patterns, political aspects and economic life.

Education is considered as the most influential agent of change in social life patterns in terms of commensality with castes, untouchability, harassment by higher castes.

4.1 Commensality

We have used commensality referring to interaction of Scheduled Castes with other castes specifically with high castes on the social auspicious and festival.

Table-4 : Commensality in festival and social auspicious of the Scheduled Castes Respondents

Education	Commensality with Higher Castes	With Equals	With Lower Caste	No. of Respondents
Less	04	10	03	17
Moderate	21	08	04	33
High	30	15	05	50
Total	**55**	**33**	**12**	**100**

Thus, the facts show that largest number 30 percent of the high-educated respondents have better commensality in festival and social auspicious with high castes people. And the lowest number 5 percent are less educated respondents having commensality with high caste. The high educated respondents have better commensality with high caste comparison to low educated.

4.2 Untouchability

Untouchability is the aspect, which effects the total social life of Scheduled Castes person in changing social environment untouchability also change.

Table-5 : Untouchability among Scheduled Castes Respondents

Education	Increase	Decrease	No Change	No. of Respondents
Less	00	13	04	17
Moderate	00	33	00	33
High	00	50	00	50
Total	**00**	**96**	**04**	**100**

Thus, the facts show that all highly educated and moderate educated respondents feel that untouchability has decreased. A few less educated respondents say that untouchability is not changed.

4.3 Harassment

Before independence Scheduled Castes suffer many type of harassment by higher caste, but after independence constitutional provisions change their situation.

Table-6: Harassment of Scheduled Caste Respondents by Higher Castes

Education	Increase	Decrease	No Change	No. of Respondents
Less	02	13	02	17
Moderate	01	32	00	33
High	06	44	00	50
Total	**09**	**89**	**02**	**100**

Thus, the fact shows that the largest segment (89 percent) of the respondents say that harassment of Scheduled Castes by higher castes has decreased.

5. Change in Political Aspects

The Constitutional safeguards have been provided to protect and to promote their interests, numerous schemes and programmes are being implemented to bring about desired changes in political conditions.

5.1 Political Awareness

After independence India is declared as welfare state so that provide many political facilities to Scheduled Castes that change their political awareness.

Table-7: Political awareness of Scheduled Caste Respondents

Education	Not aware	Less aware	Highly aware	No. of Respondents
Less	00	17	00	17
Moderate	00	30	03	33
High	00	32	18	50
Total	**00**	**79**	**21**	**100**

Thus, the facts show that every respondent is aware about politics. Majority (79 percent) of respondents are less aware, but small number highly educated (21 percent) respondents are highly aware about politics.

5.2 Voting Behaviour

After declaring about franchise, voting behaviour is an important variable that can determine their participation in politics.

Table-8: Voting Behaviour of Scheduled Castes Respondents

Education	Increase	Decrease	No Change	No. of Respondents
Less	02	13	02	17
Moderate	01	32	00	33
High	06	44	00	50
Total	**09**	**89**	**02**	**100**

Thus, the fact shows that every respondents participate in voting behavior. The largest segment of the highly educated respondents votes with independent decision.

6. Change in Economic Life

Education helps to acquire a high social status and accelerates the process of social economic mobility. It encourages not only rural to urban migration, but also accelerates the process of occupational mobility from agriculture to non-agricultural field.

Occupation is a significant variable, which plays an important role in uplifting of their social life.

Table-9 : The Occupational Change of Scheduled Caste Respondents in Past to Present Generation

Occupation	Past Generation	Present Generation	Change
Agriculture	36	00	-36
Labourer	34	05	-29
Skilled Labourer	18	09	-09
Government job	00	50	+50
Private job	00	12	+12
Business	00	24	+12
Total	**100**	**100**	

Thus, the fact shows that at present, largest segment, i.e. 50 percent respondents are engaged in government jobs as compared to none in the past in government jobs. And the lowest number (5 percent) of respondents at present are engaged in labour work. But in previous generation, 34 percent were engaged in labour work.

7. Summary and Findings

On the basis of analysis of the facts we arrive at the following findings:

1. The number of illiterates have greatly reduced among the Scheduled Castes over two generations.
2. The majority (50 percent) of the respondents are graduate or post graduate, (33 percent) are high school or intermediate and very less (17 percent) of the respondents are primary or lesser educated.
3. Majority of the respondents (78 percent) feel equal opportunities for male-female education in their families.

4. The highly educated (30 out of 50) respondents have better commensality on festival and social auspicious occasions with high castes people.
5. The majority (83 percent) of all highly and moderate educated respondents feel that untouchability has decreased.
6. Majority of respondents have less awareness about politics but a small number of highly educated respondents is highly aware about politics. Education plays a vital role in increasing awareness among Scheduled Castes.
7. All of the respondents participated in voting, a majority (56 percent) of the respondents cast their votes with independent decision, not influenced by others.
8. Due to education their traditional occupation are changing. Education is important determination that is shaping their occupations.

Compared with the studies conducted earlier, we observe the following trends, similarities and variations.

N.K. Singhi[16] has found that education is an important indicator of the social status. Education influences the process of social change among Scheduled Castes and Scheduled Tribes people. Our findings also suggest the same. Thus, it suggests a wider generalization that education plays an important role in bringing social change in the present times.

S. Patwardhan[17] has found that various groups of Scheduled Caste show a different degree of development and differential capacity to utilize the welfare schemes initiated by the government. Competition among the groups continue to acquire larger share of benefits. With the increasing urbanization and spread of education, many persons from the Scheduled Caste are now entering the ranks of the middle classes and some are even trying to reach higher ups. Our findings also suggest that highly educated respondents, having the awareness about constitutional provisions and welfare schemes, are utilizing more effectively in comparison to low educated respondents. Thus, highly educated persons among scheduled caste have achieved higher status in society.

P. N. Pandey[18] finds influence of education in social mobility and changing status identities among the Scheduled Castes, specially their rise in social hierarchy and social position mobilization and engagement in secular occupation as a result of growing more education. Our findings also suggest the same. Thus, it suggests a wider generalization that educational mobility, occupational mobility and spatial mobility can be seen among Scheduled Caste through education. Their commensal relations are also improving with other castes. They are receiving high status and are breaking the hierarchical bondage's of occupations, social intercourse, social relations etc.

M.L.Jha[19] considers that educational development and expansion among the Scheduled Castes will surely help change their traditional occupation and low levels of living standard. Our study also suggest that educational development helps in shifting from traditional occupations and low level of living standard.

This study also shows that education at least effects the nature of occupation, social, political, educational level but it can not be said clearly that the course of these changes is either by education or urbanization because of becoming the part of urban area, people are utilizing many of the urban facilities. There is no doubt many social changes are emerging among Scheduled Castes but a new type of inequality is also emerging within the Scheduled Castes themselves. So a new type of isolation can be observed among Scheduled Castes themselves which can be referred untouchability among the untouchables.

Thus we can conclude by saying that education acts as a cause and determinant of social change, education can be cause of social change and can be effected by social change, but urbanization also influences the nature of social change. Thus, the present era appears to bring social, educational, occupational and other changes in the lives of Scheduled Castes in which globalization, as a process, is also affecting all aspects of social life.

Notes and References

1. M.S.A. Rao, *Traditional Rationality and Change,* Bombay : Popular Prakashan, 1972.
2. U.N.J. Rao, *Deprived Castes in India: A Profile of Karnataka*, Allahabad : Chugh Publications, 1981.
3. S. Chitnis, "Sociology of Education", *I.C.S.S.R.'s First Survey of Research in Sociology and Social Anthropology*, Vol. III, Bombay : Popular Prakashan, 1974, pp. 166-232.
4. N. K. Singhi, *Education and Social Change*, Jaipur : Rawat Publication, 1979.
5. S. Patwardhan, *Change Among India's Harijans*, New Delhi: Orient Longman, 1973.
6. Rao, Ibid., note 2.
7. M. L. Jha, *Untouchability and Education : A Sociological Study of Attitudes,* Meerut : Namita Publication, 1973.
8. P. N. Pandey, *Education and Social Mobility*, Delhi : Daya Publishing House, 1988.
9. C. Parvathamma, *Scheduled Castes and Tribes: A Socio-Economic Survey*, New Delhi : Ashish Publishing House, 1984.
10. A. Giddens, *The Consequences of Modernity*, Stanford, C.A.: Stanford University Press, 1990.
11. S. Paswan and P. Jaideva (eds.), *Encyclopaedia of Dalits in India*, Vol 2 and 10, New Delhi : Mahere Offset Press, 2002.
12. N. K. Singhi, Ibid., note 4.

13. C. Patwardhan, Ibid., note 5.
14. M. L. Jha, Ibid., note 7.
15. Patwardhan, Ibid., note 5.
16. Singhi, Ibid., note 4.
17. S. Patwardhan, Ibid., note 5.
18. P. N. Pandey, Ibid., note 8.
19. M. L. Jha, Ibid., note 7.

****

9

Impact of Globalization and Liberalization on Zari Embroidery in India

*Surabhi Mahajan**

Globalization and liberalization have become very important and highly debatable processes world over and the Indian society is no exception to it. The nature of these processes and their impact on Indian economy as well as society form the content of serious discussions in various social science conferences, government agencies, policy makers and corporate world. The subject has assumed great significance in the light of the recent changes in the global business environment and the national economic policy changes in India. In fact, the very first objective of the Export-Import Policy (1992-97) of India has been to establish the framework for globalization of India's foreign trade. The process of globalization has been identified with the policy reforms in 1991 and the subsequent extension of these in the later years. This is the reason that globalization and liberalization are seen as twin processes in India.

1. Meaning of Globalization

The term 'globalization' means adopting a global outlook for the business and business strategies aimed at enhancing global competitiveness and mutual inter-dependence among the economies of different countries. It is a multidimensional

* Course Co-ordinator, Sportking Institute of Fashion Technology, Ludhiana (Punjab), India.

concept that refers to the transformation of trade, technology, industry and economy in a universalizing direction. It is, in fact, the attempt at the global dissemination of free market economy that is driven by the belief that the best interests of humanity are served when goods, services and finances are allowed to cross national boundaries untrammeled. Since the collapse of communism, this ideology has totally dominated world economies. Evidence of this is the fact that China, the only one remaining significant economic player that still claims to be communist, has succeeded in joining the World Trade Organization, which is the international guardian of the free market. Because the necessity for growth is a free market dogma, there is intense pressure for companies to become bigger and bigger so that they can corner a greater and greater proportion of the particular market in which they operate. This drive for growth has led to the formation of Trans-National Companies (TNCs) that are global players in the international market.

Some of the facts about them are striking. The ten largest TNCs have a total income greater than that of 100 of the world's poorest countries. Two-third of international trade is accounted for by just 500 corporations. Of the world's 100 largest economies, fifty are TNCs. For example, someone in a remote Indian village had been able to purchase a television and a video to watch various programmes as also the Western films if he likes to do so. In this way, globalization has enhanced communication with the use of sophisticated technology.

Companies which have adopted a global outlook stop thinking of themselves as national marketers. The top management and staff are involved in the planning of world-wide manufacturing facilities, marketing policies, financial flows and logistical systems. The global operating units report directly to the chief executive or executive committee, not to the head of an international division. Executives are trained in world-wide operations, not just domestic or international.

Management is recruited from many countries; components and supplies are purchased where they can be obtained at the least cost; and investments are made where the anticipated returns are the greatest.

Globalization views the entire world as a single market; it does not differentiate between domestic market and foreign markets. In other words, there is nothing like a home market and international market—there is only one market, i.e., the global market.

In fact, globalization refers to the policy of opening country's doors for foreign investors, reducing import duties and protecting the interests of foreign investors. On the other side, it also refers to the boosting up of the exports of a country and capturing the foreign markets. The basic features of the policy of globalization are as follows—

1. Minimization of government intervention in national as well as international markets.
2. Determination of exchange rates by market forces.
3. Minimization of tariff, quotas and other restrictions.
4. Equal protection to technological developments.
5. Free capital in-flow and out-flow.
6. Free movement of human labour.

Role of the government under globalization is to act as a 'pusher and challenger'. It is neither over-protective or over-supportive. It makes efforts to encourage/push the business firms to enhance their aspirations and zeal for attaining a higher level of competitiveness. Government policies aim in creating and upgrading skilled human resources, economic intelligence, infrastructure, technical know how, etc. Government encourages establishment of centres of education and training with unique excellence side by side with private endeavour in this regard. It stimulates improvements in science and technology which are integral to improving efficiency and productivity of business enterprises and support on-going innovation. Government exploits both private and public resources for building of modern and improved infrastructure such as advanced transportation, telecommunications and multimedia super corridor with advanced information technologies.

Institutions like International Monetary Fund (IMF), International Bank for Reconstruction and Development (IBRD) and World Trade Organization (WTO formely known as GATT) aim at creating free competitive atmosphere on international level.

2. Meaning of Liberalization

Liberalization refers to a process where economic policy emphasizes minimum restrictions, maximum freedom and least administrative controls on economy so that industries are kept liberalized from regulations and controls to their maximum. Only essential and priority based industries are regulated and controlled by the government. The basic features of liberalization are as follows:

1. Delicensing of industries.
2. Contraction of public sector enterprises.
3. Freedom from bureaucratic controls.
4. Encouragement to private sector.
5. Creation of healthy competition between private and public sectors.

3. Globalization and Liberalization in India

India has initiated, since August 1991, a far-reaching Structural Adjustment Program (SAP) to reduce policy-induced rigidities in the functioning of the economy and to achieve competitiveness in the international market. The SAP involves reducing state intervention in product and factor markets and correcting the import substitution bias that characterized India's industrial development strategy and policy. The policy reforms include industrial deregulation, reduction of tariffs and quantitative restrictions on imports, access to disembodied foreign technology, and liberalization of exchange rate and foreign direct investment policies. The primary objective of policy changes has been to improve the efficiency of the manufacturing sector through increased competitive pressure and access to imported inputs at international prices.

India's international business has been confined mostly to exports. Although some developing countries like South Korea and Taiwan, whose economic position had not been better than that of India when India started planned development, have made substantial investments in other countries, Indian companies have not made any significant foreign investment so far. Although Government of India's policy has been one of encouraging foreign investment by Indian companies, subject to certain conditions, several factors like the domestic economic policy and the domestic economic situation have been deterrents to foreign investment by Indian companies.

By restricting the areas of operation and growth, the government policy seriously constrained the potential of Indian companies to make a foray into the foreign countries through investment. Added to this was the attraction of the protected domestic market which was, in many cases, a seller's market which made the Indian companies to ignore the foreign markets.

Soon after the installation of the Congress Government, headed by Sri P. V. Narsimha Rao as Prime Minister on June 21, 1991, a series of measures of economic reforms were undertaken. The measures were unleashed in quick succession and were intended to unshackle the economy from the cobwebs of unnecessary controls to liberalize the economy so as to bring about global integration, to remove restrictions on direct foreign investment and also to free the domestic entrepreneur from the restrictions of MRTP Act. Changes initiated in various fields in this respect are given below–

3.1 Changes in India's Foreign Trade Policy

The then Union Cabinet Minister, Mr. P. Chidambaram announced a major over-haul of trade policy on July 4, 1991. The changes were–

i. Suspension of each compensatory support.

ii. An enlarged and uniform rep rate of 30 per cent of FOB value.

iii. Abolition of all supplementary licences except in the case of small scale sector and producers of life saving drugs / equipment.

iv. Abolition of unlisted OGI.

v. Removal of all import licensing for capital goods and raw materials except for a small negative list in 3 years.

Though the first major attempt of liberalization was done by Rajiv Gandhi Government, it could not take its own course in later years.

3.2 Changes in Industrial Policy

The new industrial policy was announced on July 24, 1991. The baisc features of this policy are given below–

a) Industrial licensing

i. Industrial licensing will be abolished for all projects except for a small list of industries related to security and strategic concerns, social reasons, hazardous chemicals and over-riding environmental reasons and items of cities consumptions. Industries reserved for the small scale sector will continue to be so reserved.

ii) In projects where imported capital goods are required, automatic clearance will be given.

iii. In location other than cities of more than 10 lakh population, there will be no requirement of obtaining industrial approvals from the central government except for industries subject to compulsory licensing.

iv. All existing registration schemes will be abolished and the entrepreneurs will hence forth only be required to file an information memorandum on new projects and substantial expansions.

b) Foreign Investment

i. Approval will be given for direct foreign investment upto 51 percent foreign equity in higher priority industries.

ii. To provide access to international markets, majority foreign equity holdings upto 51 per cent equity will be allowed for trading companies primarily engaged in export activities.

c) Foreign Technology Agreement

i. Automatic permission will be given for foreign technology agreements in higher priority industries upto a lump sum payment of Rs. 1 crore. 5 percent royalty for domestic sales and 8 percent for exports, subject to total payment of 8 percent of sales over a ten year period from date of agreement or 7 years from commencement of production.

ii. No permission will be necessary for hiring of foreign technicians, foreign testing of indigenously developed technologies.

d) Public Sector

i. Private and public sector will be allowed entry in areas not reserved for either.

ii. Sick public units will be referred to BIFR for revival/ rehabilitation.

iii. Some shares of public sector will be disinvested.

e) MRTP Act

i. The MRTP Act will be amended to remove the threshold

limits of assets in respect of MRTP companies and dominant undertakings.

ii. Emphasis will be placed on controlling and regulating monopolistic, restrictive and unfair trade practices.

iii. Necessary comprehensive amendments will be made in the MRTP Act.

3.3 Devaluation of the Rupee

On July 1 and July 3, 1991, the Reserve Bank of India in two successive announcements effected exchange rate adjustment lowering the value of the rupee by about 18-19 percent with respect to major currencies.

3.4 Convertibility of Rupee

The government announced to introduce LERMS (Liberalized Exchange Rate Management System) in order to protect the interests of the exporters and control the illegal 'Hawala Bazar' activities, through 1992-93 budget proposals and made rupee partially convertible. In seriation, rupee was made fully convertible in Current Account in the budget proposals of 1994-95. As per declaration 40 percent of gross earned foreign exchange can be converted.

3.5 Expansion of Private Sector

The government wants to promote private efficiency.

i. The number of industries reserved for public sector has been reduced from 17 to 8.

ii. Investment limit for small industries has been increased. (Now it is 1 crore).

iii. The producers are free to choose the products of their own choice.

iv. Ceiling on expansion of productive capacity has been renewed.

Thus economic policy in the decade of 90's paved the way

for liberalization, privatization and globalization in Indian economy. By adopting liberal approach towards licensing, controls, quota fixation and tariffs, the government has started on era of cumulative losses, the government is promoting privatization and disinvestment in PSU's. The government is providing adequate facilities to the private enterprises and multinational corporations due to which the national markets have expanded into global markets.

The new economic policy of India is expected to encourage the globalization of Indian business. The increasing domestic competition is compelling many companies to pursue globalization vigorously. The liberalization of policy towards foreign technology and collaborations is enabling Indian companies to upgrade their production facilities or to establish new facilities which help them enter or expand the foreign market. A number of companies have thus increased their foreign business.

A number of Indian companies are also setting up units abroad, either alone or in collaboration with foreign firms. Indian companies have also been acquiring firms in foreign countries. More and more Indian firms have been taking advantage of the international sourcing by becoming suppliers of parts and components to companies abroad. For example, the recent recession in the Indian automobile industry has encouraged several component manufacturers to seek buyers abroad.

Technological and marketing tie-ups with foreign will play a major role in globalization of the Indian business. While many foreign firms are interested in such collaborations for sourcing supplies for the foreign markets, many other foreign firms would like to have such collaborations for business in both the Indian and foreign markets.

Indian business, however, encounters the following problems in globalization:

1. Policy and procedural problems.
2. Infrastructural bottlenecks.
3. Resource constraints.
4. High domestic costs.
5. Lack of experience in managing business abroad.
6. Limited R and D and marketing research.

Although a number of companies are planning to substantially expand their international business, a true global orientation is yet to set in.

4. Impact of Globalization & Liberalization on Zari Embroidery

The processes of globalization and liberalization have enormously expanded the scope of the private sector in India. Now only six industries are reserved for the public sector. Even in some of these industries, selective entry of the private sector is allowed. Industrial licensing is confined to 15 industries which account for only 15 percent of the value added in the manufacturing sector. The MRTP regulations pertaining to entry and growth have been scrapped. The private enterprises can now enter and grow in most of the industries. Further, automatic approval of foreign investment upto 51 percent and foreign technology agreements are permitted for 35 priority industries. These industries account for about 50 percent of the value added in the manufacturing sector.

As a result of globalization and liberalization, there has been enormous changes in Indian economy. Investment has been surging, competition has been increasing, growth rate has been picking up, supply has been expanding in quantity and variety, industrial efficiency has been improving and exports have been accelerating. Globalization and liberalization have given an enormous boost to private investment in the industrial sector. In 1990-91, the years prior to liberalization, the total capital mobilized by the private corporate sector by equity issues was Rs. 1,261 crores. Assuming a debt equity ratio of 1 : 3 the total investment that would have taken place in the private corporate sector in that year would be less than Rs. 3,000 crores including the foreign capital. In 1994-95, i.e., within four years since globalization and liberalization the equity capital mobilized increased to about Rs. 27,621 crores. Including the foreign capital, the total investment could be over Rs. 65,000 crores. In the 1970s, the average annual amount of capital raised by the corporate sector from the primary market was below Rs. 100 crores. In 1995, a single organization (IDBI) had an issue of over Rs. 2,000 crores which was over subscribed.

The processes of globalization and liberalization in India has adversely affected the Indian industries, particularly the small scale industries. Number of small scale industries have closed down leading to increased unemployment. Many Indian industries have not been able to compete with multi national companies (MNCs). The latter have taken over many Indian industries. The emphasis on privatization due to pressures of globalization and liberalization in India has put the under-privileged sections in disadvantageous position as the benefits of these processes have increased hiatus between haves and have-nots.

In fact, the doubts were raised in the beginning about the adverse and negative impact of the processes of globalization and liberalization on the under-privileged sections in India because the state feels helpless in protecting their interests in private sector. The benefits of globalization and liberalization have not been equally distributed among various sections of Indian society.

The artisans and workers in many industries have been rendered jobless due to huge inflow of foreign goods in Indian markets closing down many small scale units. Zari embroidery, unlike other embroideries, has been able to sustain itself successfully in national and international market in spite of tough competition from countries like Pakistan and Bangladesh.

On the contrary, globalization and liberalization have increased the demand not only for heavy zari work on garments like *lehangas, shararas* and saris meant for special occasions and marriages in national market but also for light work on garments like suits and skirts etc. meant for casual wear abroad.

The introduction of zardozi in casual clothes has led to a further increase in its demand. Its demand has not only increased in domestic market but has also extended considerably in international market. The craft in other countries has become almost a part of the daily routine wear. Sometimes designs and specifications for raw material were faxed to the exporters in India with the result that the use of such raw materials like ribbons, beads, crystals, silk thread instead of the normal gold and silver thread has become much common now-a-days. This kind of work was done similarly as the gold and silver work and zardoz call it by the term zardozi though no zari i.e., gold thread is being used for it. In fact, now for these craftsmen, everything that they work on a cloth stretched on wooden frame or karchob is termed as zardozi whether it incorporates zari or not. This kind of work is more common in international markets on articles like skirts, scarfs, jackets, shirts etc. though it can be seen to a lesser extent in domestic market.

There is clear change seen in demand for zardozi items in domestic and international markets as it has increased manifold. This is due to the increase in popularity of items of zardozi. Majority of zardoz have also confirmed it. The popularity is increasing day by day with the increase in purchasing power of customers and the craze for more decoration besides the use of this embroidery in daily wear items also. This increase in popularity is also evident in international markets and India has already become a leading country in zardozi exports, earning a good amount of foreign currency every year. This was confirmed by government officials in Directorate of Industries, Government of Uttar Pradesh, Bareilly. However, this industry is facing many challenges in export such as technological backwardness, uneconomic size of the production units, infrastructure problems, irregular supply of raw materials of requisite specification, frequent hike in administered prices of key inputs, heavy burden of taxes and duties, high incidence of interest rates and low productivity following excessive labour protection leading to price disadvantage limits of export efforts. Besides, delivery schedule is also not maintained due to transport bottlenecks, power shortage, labour unrest, lack of port facilities etc. which make the situation more worse. All these challenges and difficulties require the immediate attention of the government so that zardozi can continue to stand on firm footing in the local as well as in the foreign markets.

In the apparel industry, globalization of production activities has meant that a garment can be designed in New York, produced by using the fabric made in the Republic of Korea, cut in Hong Kong, and assembled in China, for eventual distribution in the United Kingdom or the United States. Frontiers of nation-states no longer determine the business strategies of producer firms or the purchasing strategies of large distribution networks. The main factors which have contributed to the globalization of world apparel industry are the labour-intensive nature of apparel production technology, the loss of comparative cost advantage of developed countries, dramatic decline in transport and communication costs, search for production sites with lower labor costs, and the shift in apparel exports from more restricted to less restricted among the developing countries due to the discriminatory nature of the restrictions imposed by the Multifibre Arrangement (MFA). It is reported that roughly half of the total production capacity in the apparel industry has shifted from developed countries to less developed countries over the past three decades. The fundamental factor which explains this relocation movement in the global apparel industry and the emergence of new producing countries is the international differences in hourly wage costs in the clothing industry.

Apparel is India's leading export product and achieved rapid growth in the late 1980s and the first half of the 1990s. However, India's share of world apparel exports has not risen since 1994. The immediate cause is apparently the slowdown in the import growth of India's major markets, namely, the United States and the EU. A more significant observation is that the apparel industry has remained outside the industrial reforms of the 1990s.

India is at present a niche player in the low-value market segment based on cotton fabrics and for seasonal and fashion garments. This reflects India's comparative advantage in cotton cloth and its flexibility advantage in meeting small orders. Access to imported inputs, fabric, trimmings, and accessories appear to have become easier with their removal from the restricted list in India.

However, the processes of globalization and liberalization have not been able to improve the socio-economic conditions of zardoz and those engaged in apparel industry. The profit of thekedars and shopkeepers has increased manifold due to export orders. However, there has not been much difference in the earnings of actual artisans. Their condition is still very pathetic and miserable, they are being exploited and have no way out to improve their lot.

****

10

Globalization and Agrarian Social Structure : An Empirical Inquiry of Farmers in Western U.P.

*Malti Phogat**

1. Introduction

Globalization and farmers discourse continues since the recent wave of liberalization, structural adjustment and economic reforms have started in India about more than a decade ago (in 1991). This opened the doors of Indian economy to the world economy and vice a versa. In case of agricultural sector the debate has been going on how and in what manner Indian agriculture is going to be affected by these reforms, liberalization and consequent policies. Some have been arguing in favour of it that agricultural sector will be benefited, there will be diversification of agriculture and ultimately that will boost the production which will positively effect the Indian farmers and the rural population in general. On the other hand others are arguing strongly against globalization and have been indicating that farmers and rural population in India is going to be adversely affected. It is feared that the multinational corporations by way of free flow of goods, capital and services will grab not only the industrial resources but also the agricultural sector, agri-business and probably result is to pauperization of Indian agriculturists, small farmers and rural labour. Most of such positive and negative apprehension have

* Department of Sociology, N.A.S. College (CCS University), Meerut, India.

been indicated either on the basis of possible implications of the policies that have been followed by the state, logical derivations and in some cases lessons drawn from some other parts of the world where such policy reforms have already gone into. But there are not many cases where the empirical realities from the point of actual recipients i.e. the farmers have been high lighted.

The very impact on a certain section or sections may begin by knowing how they acquire knowledge or awareness, make perceptions and actually feel the effect on work and life. Thus the present paper aims to understand perceptions and understanding of globalization in rural India, the impact felt so far on agriculture by the farmers themselves. The arguments for and against i.e. negative and positive consequence for rural society in general and farmers in particular, and more importantly examined the core issues through the findings of an actual empirical inquiry undertaken in north India, western U.P. which is largely known as the heartland of agriculture in upper Ganga Doab. The empirical inquiry has focused upon the issues of awareness and consequently the impact on general agrarian relations. Before the findings are presented to actually contribute to the debate, the related issues are taken up as reflected from select evidence from voluminous literature growing on globalization in India.

2. Perceptions and Understanding of Globalization

Globalization appears to be an economic phenomenon indicating a strong international interconnection, which refers to a situation wherein industrial and commercial companies have free flow of goods and financial institutions increasingly operate freely across transnational borders. This goes in hand with an increase in mergers and acquisition of industrial, commercial and financial enterprises, leading to an increasing global role of large, multinational companies and lessening of the role of individual identity of nation states.[1] If globalization is understood in its meaning as a process of interaction and transference between preexisting units, in its other (or reverse) meaning globalization level and thus it affects the systems as much as it affects the identity of units.[2] Some others see globalization as primarily and economic phenomenon involving increasing interaction or integration of economic systems through the growth in international trade, investment and capital flows. This means the opening of the national economies to the world by removing barriers against free flow of trade, investment, information technology and the consumer get interrelated.[3] Thus globalization of economies of the world requires the emergence of competitive milieu both in the relation between the nation states as also for the internal interactions of each of these nations. It was believed that globalization will make the economies more efficient by breaking down protectionism (even with in a nation) and thereby making then competitive milieu a characteristic feature of the processes.[4]

One of the known sociologists of late twentieth century[5] considers globalization as the intensification of world wide social relations which link distant locations in such a way that local happenings are shaped by events occurring many miles away and vice-versa. This is a dialectical process because such local happenings may move in an observe direction from the very distantiated relations that shape them. Thus local transformation becomes as much a part of the globalization as the extension of social connections across time and space. Another way of viewing globalization suggests that it focuses on new international division of labour which is developing across the world, forcing capital to migrate to labour surplus economies which results in recession and increasing unemployment in advanced industrialized societies. A tendency which also indicates decentralization of capital which is made possible by modern technology process and manufacturing can be set up in locations enjoying the advantages of cheap labour and raw material or market for the products. This feature of scattered decentralization has been made possible by modern communication technology, which allows exercising effective and flexible control over its far-flung and diverse operations.

The world system also appears to be undergoing major shifts in the balance of economic power, the modern capitalist class of advanced nations or multinational corporation are facing a future full of uncertainties, what to say of economically less developed economies. The opened situation of the world system today provides the prephery seize this movement and the world systems will undergo radical change. Sociologists noted that cultures and cultural frontiers are perceived and interpreted in novel ways and globalization has mode the quest for universalism, a prominent feature of modernity. Thereby the modern world systems are caught in post modern moral gridlock. It is further important to recognize that cultural identities are both generated and constructed in post modern globalism. Despite universalistic and homogenizing tendencies that reinforce one dimensionality of man, allows space to various groups to articulate their perception, understanding and interpretations. Thus globalization, far from reducing the world system into a monolithic and functionalist cultural order, accommodates plurality of cultures... Between and across nations.

Thus globalization apparently looking as an economic phenomenon entails making economies of individual nations open to all other nations, essentially emphasizing on free flow of capital and goods across boundaries; to ensure this free flow of capital, goods and financies and technology nations are required to make amendments in policies, tariff rates and remove all related restrictions for integration of economies. The implications impinge upon the political systems for making change in the policies. Whereas in democracies diverse ideologies may hasten and infact hastening somewhere or slowing down elsewhere the free regime that is required. In social terms indicates intensification of social relations. By linking distant locations and people that local happenings are affected and shapped by events occurring at far away corners on the glob. On the other hand it is also creating a dialicties as local happenings and people with differing ideologies may affect the quantum and speed of this integration and interaction.

As much as economic and political, it is clubbed with technologies, much more with information technologies, the globalization is affecting cultures of societies. Now the emerging scenario suggests that cultures and cultural frontiers are perceived and interpreted in noval ways and globalization has made the quest possible for universalism, which is a feature of modernity. Thus some transformation in existing cultures of individual societies is inevitable. Thereby the world systems are caught in a post modern new moral grid lock and cultural identities are constructed and are being generated in the from post modernism i.e. globalism. Despite universalistic and homogenizing tendencies that reinforce one dimensionality of man it also, allows various groups to articulate their perceptions, understandings and interpretations. Thus the globalization is influencing the world systems in several dimensions of social man in grouping despite it appears to show one dimensionality of man by creating universalism.

3. The Indian Scenario: Impact on Agriculture

India accounts for about a third of the world's absolute poor therefore the nature of her integration with international economy has critical implications. India has been relatively a closed economy and a mixed economy of private and public enterprise during first four decades of its independence. The state has played a key role in attempting to bring about transformation through policies, including internal and external, and achievements have been underpinned by both domestic and international pressures, to emphasize upon market forces and to keep in view both growth and poverty.[6]

India's signing the GATT agreement in 1994, put Indian agriculture into the frame, work of global competition and under the rule of global market. However, the issue of the competitive Indian agriculture has been carried on in a narrow context, ignoring major questions such as global commodity prospects in terms of prices and their stability/instability, movement of the domestic and world market prices and prices of agricultural and non-agricultural goods with in the country.[7] There is apparently opening of doors for exports and imports including that of agricultural produce which is placing the farmers in a competitive milieu either described as a large, closed and protected economy, but now opening foreign investment in industry and agriculture. The share of foreign investment in agricultural sector has been limited so far thereby export of agricultural produce is still small whereas it should have increased many fold. This situation of ideally export led growth should have been labour absorbing and skill enhancing and making the labour market more flexible. This required state provisions for redundancy and retraining programmes to minimize any adverse socio-economic effects and the re-absorption of labour in a growing economy but the same has not been coming up in a significant way.[8] Requiring commercial mechanization of agriculture and all forms of agribusiness, even food self-sufficiency (which is of course available in surplus despite famines in some areas) agrarian labour and rural employment may be gravely jeopardized. It is a fact, which is to be accepted because of globalization so far.

Evidence also indicates that there has been a decline in the pervasiveness of traditional relationships, whether Jajmani or labour relations. Both dominant land holders and labourers observe concerns that extent of such relationships are no longer sustainable.[9] Of course some little ownership of land among rural poor have increased productivity and wages, but on the other hand it has been observed that small, indeed negative difference between government stipulated/minimum wages and lesser importance of land distribution to the poor is reducing the importance of these two factors-wages and productivity.[10] It is further observed that new economic policy may effect the poor, particularly rural poor adversely and thereby register a rise in poverty and unemployment in rural area.[11]

By way of treaties and agreements during globalization, the rights of genetic resources of the Indian farmers do not figure anywhere in the GATT exchange. The new world gave wealth in plants and received disease collection of rich biodiversity in India are treated as the same as collection of jojoba. Secondly at the intellectual level farmers' knowledge in the Third World (including India) is treated as not needing protection whereas western corporate knowledge is treated as needing protection. The main problem with farmers as construed in the F.A.O commission is that the farmers do not have place for negotiating biodiversity rights and determining patterns of biodiversity utilization. The system of compensation through aid and assistance for the exploitation of these resources is in appropriate, insufficient and undignified.[12] The global reorganization of agriculture and food is proceeding rapidly in East Asia under the auspices of the indigenous firms......this process is being promoted, in part, by increasing foreign direct investment in agri-food firms (not by individual farmers), like in Japan and east Asia.[13] But that is perhaps not happening in India. World trade in agriculture interms of macro-economic stabilization combined with fiscal adjustments and structural reforms in India have of course constrained and have significant impact on agriculture, particularly in terms of domestic prices of inputs and outputs closer to world prices. Uruguay Round and Dunkel Text expected inevitably to change the structure of relative prices for agricultural commodities and inputs. These developments may have serious implications and consequences for India, not only in other trades but also for agriculture traditional export, which originate from agricultural items like tea, coffee, tobacco, spices... etc., have always beer an important source of earning foreign exchange. Indian share in world market has rather reduced. Exportable production is residual as the difference between actual domestic production and estimated domestic consumption. When up the volumes of exports it can exercise a strong influence on domestic prices of those items, as there are no longer any quantitative restrictions of agricultural exports or imports. Despite all this India's position is marginal in exports of these items.

The common agriculture policy is built along two dimensions—the convergence of production ad change as well as to the adjustment of European agricultural sector's demands of globalization.[14] Increasing demand of labour in construction and other sectors in this regime has led to increase in wages in agricultural which is needed, started destroying natural resources and degradation of farm land to the extent that substance farmers are not able to produce even as much as they used to produce earlier[15] while 1980's witnessed a wide spread acceleration in per male agricultural worker productivity in many states.[16] It is also observed that new policy linked the prices of inputs but has also increased productivity.[17] Which is not always true.

Further the globalization regime is pushing for with drawl of subsides from agricultural sector, there is very likelyhood to decline of productivity due to lesser capital availability with majority of small and middle farmers.[18] The export oriented agricultural economy is to serve the rich farmers and exporters, encourage horticulture and exportable crops.

There is an important issue of patents, some agricultural items are being patented in U.S.A. whereas those the basically Indian e.g. Basmati Rice. On this issue the organization of farmers are also divided—one arguing for it and the other arguing that farmers loose right to modify seeds and reuse thereby they will dependent upon the multinational corporations or corporate enterprises for requirements of seeds for commercial farming. The large requirement of seeds will not be met by these, and prices will be beyond the approach of small and middle farmers therefore larger part of land will be used for lesser productivity. There are restrictions on sale of seeds from farmer to farmer which at present contribute to more than 60 percent, the public sector or private enterprise met only 32 percent requirements. This way also the new global regime will jeopardize the situation and average and small farmers would always be at a loss.

4. The Empirical Inquiry and its Findings

The empirical study was undertaken in two villages in Bulandshahr district of Western Uttar Pradesh. The district area and the villages lie in the fertile plains of upper Ganga-Yamuna Doab. One of the villages is situated in the proximity (3 Km) of the district headquarter town whereas the other village lies comparatively in the interior where lesser facilities of transport and communication are available. One caste composition and occupations the villages are almost similar. 100 heads of farmers' households from each of the two villages were selected out of the 398 (i.e. out of 200 and 198 respectively). 100 each (i.e. 200) respondents (heads of house holds) were selected alternatively by selecting a random number in each case. Initially a few case studies were developed on the basis of observations and informal interviews which provided the possible aspects of background, awareness, perception and impact of globalization. There after data were collected from the respondents with the help of an unstructured schedule which was used more or less like an interview guide.

The study has basically focused upon the three main concerns—the awareness and impact of globalization of farmers and the social consequence of globalization in general on the agrarian relations. On these issues the findings of empirical inquiry may now be depicted here:

1. Awareness about globalization among farmers is more (60percent) in the proximity village than in the interior village (40percent); proportionately awareness is more among farmers of higher castes than of the lower castes; awareness is comparatively more among the farmers of younger age group (36-45). Than the older ones in the interior village whereas more awareness has been found in older age group in the proximit village; more of the middle farmers are aware than the smaller and bigger farmers in both the villages; farmers with other subsidiary occupations are proportionately more aware than those, whose sole occupation is agriculture.
2. Among the farmers who are aware of the globalization T.V., radio, newspaper, magazines and interpersonal interaction (group discussion) are the main sources of bringing about awareness; in the urban proximity village T.V. and radio come out to be more effective means for creating the awareness whereas in the interior village newspaper and interpersonal interaction act as major sources of awareness for majority: sole farmers acquire awareness more through interpersonal interaction where as those with other subsidiary occupations become aware through other sources namely news papers, radio and T.V.
3. Among the farmers who understand globalization, there are different perceptions—globalization as new government policy, as Dunkal proposal, and globalization as a process of opening Indian economy to the world. Majority of higher caste farmers process whereas majority of lower caste farmers understand it as a process of global economy, whereas less educated understand it as a government policy; farmers whose sole occupation is agriculture understand globalization as a government policy whereas those with other subsidiary occupations understand globalization more properly as a global process of economy.

4. Majority of farmers (86percent) who know about globalization in both the villages feel that during the period of globalization (since 1991) the cost of agricultural technology has been increasing, very less (14 percent) say that not much change has occurred and remaining others not aware.
5. Majority of farmers (68 percent) feel that now new seeds are necessary for more production, but only a smaller segment (28 percent) feel that these are made available at government stores and a larger segment (32 percent) say it is not private seed companies are supplying seeds but those are also not available to most of them.
6. Most of the farmers (80 percent) feel that prices of seeds, fertilizers and pesticides have increased during this period 1990's.
7. All farmers feel that the government is reducing subsides on these inputs under the new policies, which they perceive is emerging under the pressure of world powers. At the national level it has happened several times that the state has proposed large reduction is subsidies but political lobbies representing the farmers' interests pressed on the government and there by large cuts were reduced to smaller cuts in the subsides but at least some cut has been done which has increased the prices of agricultural inputs.
8. A majority of the farmers (68 percent) feel that the globalization is increasing the exports of agricultural produce while a small number of farmers negate this. But most of them do not understand how is it going on and feel that they are not benefited by all that.
9. A large number (79 percent) of those who understand globalization feel that all these policies (of globalization) are compelling the farmers, particularly small farmers, to adopt some other subsidiary occupations as agriculture is becoming less profitable.

10. A large majority (more than 90 percent) find that increasing use of fertilizers and pesticides which is necessary, is reducing the fertility of land and the production is decreasing. Further, this increasing use of fertilizers and pesticides is be coming harmful for the health of the people and the environment.
11. Most of the farmers feel that the present process requires new varieties of existing crops and new crops, thus some change is occurring in the cropping pattern e.g. vegetable growing.
12. The farmers are becoming aware of the fact that some foreign companies (MNCs) are coming to India, which will have an effect but they have not help the farmers in any way like providing seeds and other inputs. Of course, they acknowledge hearing such things.
13. Majority of the farmers (above 60 percent) find that labour wages have increased during the globalization regime and also availability of labour for agricultural operations is becoming lesser.
14. As a matter of social consequence the interpersonal and intergroup relations are undergoing change like dependency of farmers on each other i.e. their mutual dependency and mutual interactions are decreasing; mutual dependency and interaction between farmers and landless people are also declining in quantitative as well as in the qualitative terms. That indicates some degree of isolation is emerging between farmers to farmers and farmers to labouerers and thereby indicating that the village intergroup harmony is on the decline.

5. Conclusion

We began with the understanding of globalization as a process of integration of Indian economy with the economic of the world wide states. In basically began with measures of removing restrictions on free flow of trade-business and capital, the general rules for this came up in several documents like the Dunkal Draft and the GATT to which India has also become a signatory. This entailed structural adjustments, policy reforms and a liberalization regime in India too. Large segment of population of India lives in villages and larger part of it depends directly or indirectly on agriculture therefore this large segment has been a matter of concern of all discussions and writings on globalization. The writings have also shown concerns for effects on the system a whole. Several issues have emerged from these concerns. The empirical findings suggest and confirm some of the fears indicated in the debates on consequences of globalization on the rural society in India in general and the farmers in particular which impinge upon some changing scenario of agrarian relations.

1. The larger part of farmers are aware but still a segment is not therefore perceiving what globalization brings for them is differentially distributed. The earlier apprehensions have not taken into consideration such awareness.
2. The small farmers appear to grow and simultaneously making up some jobs and or subsidiary occupations in fact suggests it is compelling the out flow of rural population towards other sectors for substance. The fears of this variety were indicated in some of the earlier writings, as globalization to be understood as a process of transformation and effecting the identity of units (Bartelson, 2000:186). The identity of rural community is going through transformation is getting confirmed.
3. The awareness of globalization is largely coming through sources of mass media namely radio, television and news papers, but the empirical inquiry suggests that in a large measure it flows through interpersonal communication; more so through the persons keeping frequent rural-urban contacts. Even otherwise the less availability of the means

of mass communication and their lesser use (e.g. due to lack of fundamental facilities like electricity) the social change in terms of communication and its response is limited otherwise globalization appears to bring change.

4. The rural-urban proximity is found to create awareness differently among large and small farmers the urban proximity giving rise to more awareness among small farmers whereas in the interior large farmers are in touch more with out side world. Thus in the interior rural social structure more of a traditional agrarian relations continue therefore lesser change, as expected, is observable. It was indicated that large farmers are likely to be benefited appears to be true in the interior village agrarian structure but urban proximity does so for small farmers as well.
5. As far as prices of commodities are concerned it was indicated that so far the question of stability or instability has been carried on in a narrow context[19] that appear to be coming true in the empirical situations.
6. The share of foreign capital investment in agriculture has been limited and agricultural export was small[20] and thereby role of large corporations (MNCs) would grow, the empirical findings also suggest this very limited role in providing new seeds for more production and increasing productivity.
7. It was also feared that there has been a decline in the pervasiveness of traditional relationships whether in Jajman or labour relations.[21] The empirical findings also indicates the decline in these traditional relationships which was hitherto known as a unique feature of the traditional agrarian relations in India.
8. The question of rights of genetic resources of farmers did not figure in the international agreements which needed protection and thereby create problems for Indian farmers.[22]

Though the empirical finding concretely do not indicate that because the farmers largely still do not have these but at their cognitive level they are afraid of snatching such rights.

9. It was also observed that the reform policies would push for withdrawal of subsides and thereby like in the prices of inputs.[23] The empirical findings suggest that though withdrawal of subsides is small and gradual but the hike in prices of inputs is observable, in some items many fold. This is adversely effecting the farmers, small farmers therefore finding agriculture uneconomic and this scenario is pushing them towards out side where they may further fear to be reduced to unskilled labour force.
10. Last but not the least, the social consequence for the agrarian social structure is observable in breaking up of farmer-to-farmer relationship. Farmer-labour relations are loosening i.e. to say the harmony of agrarian relations is declining. This is also observable in terms of nature and increasing quantity of conficts and crimes, that globalization has promoted this process of disharmonizing of agrarian relations. Whatever way the globalization and the reforms that followed are stressing the agrarian relations for change. It is clear causes of agrarian distress were mainly a remarkable shift in cropping pattern, input prices rising fast and the rural finance institutions (RFIS) not keeping pace with the expenditure on inputs as a result farmers take recourse to the no formal sources of credit and trapped in a vicious circle of debt. RFIS has failed do deliver credit when it was needed the most, therefore continuous fallen in farmer's position.

Notes and References

1. Paul Bairoch, "The Constituent Economic Principles of Globalization in Historical Perspectives: Myths and

Realities", *International Sociology*, Vol. 15, No. 2, 2002, pp. 197-214.

2. Jens Bartelson, "There Concepts of Globalization", *International Sociology*, Vol. 15, No. 2, 2002, pp. 18-19.
3. Jyotsna Rajput, "Globalization and Emerging Trends in Industrial Development", *Yojna*, Vol. 45 (March), 2001, pp. 35-37.
4. Jyotsna Pimpley, "Communication Identities in a Competitive Milieu" paper presented in the XXI All Indian Sociological Conference, New Delhi, J.N.U., Dec. 19-21, 1994,
5. Anthony Giddens, "The Consequences of Modernity", Cambridge Polity Press, p. 64; quoted in Wilenius, Mark : "1999 : Sociological Modernity and Globalization of Environmental Change", *International Sociology*, Vol. 14, No. 1, 1990, pp. 33-57.
6. Sumit Roy, "Globalization, Structural Changes and Poverty : Conceptual and Policy Issues", *Economic and Political Weekly*, Vol. XXXII, No. 33-34, 1997, pp. 2117-27.
7. Succha Singh Gill and Jasvinder Singh Brar, "Global Market and Competitiveness of Indian Agriculture", *Economic and Political Weekly*, Vol. XXXI, No. 32, pp. 2167-27.
8. Sumit Roy, Op. Cit., note 6.
9. Davnluri Venkateshwarlu and Da Lucia Corta, "Unfree Relations and Familization Agricultural Labour in A.P. 1970-95", *Rural Labour Relations in India*, 1999.
10. C.B.P. Srivastava, *Globalization-Indian and The World Changing Scenario*, New Delhi : Kitab Mahal, 1997.
11. N. Raghunath Reddy and Hanumantha Rao, "Rural Development in Andhra Pradesh : An Historical Perspective," *The Journal of Peasant Studies*, Vol. 15, No. 4, 1996, pp. 467-89

12. Vandana Shiva, "Farmers' Right, Biodiversity and International Treaties", *Economic and Political Weekly*, Vol. XXVII, No. 14, 1993, pp. 30-32.

13. Raymond and Philip, "The Role of Asian Transitional and Corporations in Evolving Asian Agri Food Systems", paper presented in the XIV World Congress of Sociology, Montreal (Canada), July-Aug, 1998.

14. Magadalini, "The Effect of Globalization in the Agricultural Sector", XIV World Congress of Sociology, Montreal (Canada), July-Aug., 1998.

15. Agarwal and Narain, "Modern Agriculture and Development", *Indian Journal of Agricultural Economics*, Vol. 53, No. 3, 1989, pp. 302.

16. G. S. Bhalla and Gurmail Singh, "Recent Developments in Agriculture : A State Level Analysis", *Economic and Political Weekly*, Vol. XXXII, No. 13, 1997, pp. 1050-55.

17. Desai and Namboodri, "Determinants of Total Factor Productivity in Indian Agriculture", *Economic and Political Weekly*, Vol. XXXIII, April, 1998, p. 199.

18. Reddy and Despande, "Input Subsidies : Whither the Direction of Policy Changes", *Indian Journal of Agricultural Economics*, Vol. 47, No. 3, 1992, p. 37.

19. Succha Singh Gill and Jasvinder Singh Brar, Op. Cit., note 7.

20. Sumit Roy, Op. Cit., note 6.

21. Davnluri Venkateshwarlu and Da Lucia Corta, Op. Cit., note 9.

22. Vandana Shiva, Op. Cit., note 12.

23. Reddy and Despande, Op. Cit., note 18.

****

11

Globalization and its Impact on Transfer of Knowledge : Cultural Perspective

Rajul Datt**,
Amit Bhardwaj and**
Ajay Singh***

1. Globalization

When business exceeds the local focus, the management begins to recognize the global focus. Thus, business now becomes global orientation. It is brought by:

- The globe has shrinked and become one due to best means of communication.
- Video and telecommunication : There is no problem of sound and vision throughout the globe due to television.
- Advanced technology caters to the global market. Global brands, their production, finance and location are all now globalized.
- Now, companies have developed global attitude in business.

2. Transition to Globalization

In the present century, transition to the global society took place due to increasing science and technology. Thus, all aspects

* Head, Department of Management & Business Studies, Meerut Institute of Engineering & Technology, Meerut, India

** Lecturer, Department of Management & Business Studies, Meerut Institute of Engineering & Technology, Meerut, India

*** Lecturer, Department of Management & Business Studies, Meerut Institute of Engineering & Technology, Meerut, India

of our life on this planet are changing into a process of globalization through constant change. Now, no individual can monopolize in economics, commerce, and trade and in industry decisions.

Economics and commerce are far exceeding and transcending national barriers as they are rapidly becoming global.

The environment has also become global. For example, attention of ozone layer or deforestation or pollution has now become more important and assumed global dimensions.

The communication is the most important thing in the globalization. Information and technology, internet interaction, e-mail, satellite technology and breaking of the space barrier are the main sources of globalization.

Now millions of people throughout the world can concentrate their attention on one single event (TV/Video) at a single moment of time, making us global citizens. A new kind of civilization is developing throughout the world.

The competition now is no longer in the national market but it has become global. For example, USA monopoly in automobile market has decreased as the production facilities in other countries are relatively cheaper.

In present era, most of the radical changes are brought about by globalization.

A company first starts its international business by exporting first and then by subsidiaries abroad. After becoming an international company it can then turn into a multinational company before finally becoming a global one.

3. Challenges and Impacts of Globalization

Challenges to be faced by the business world in India and abroad, i.e. global economy include the following:

- The challenges of survival due to fast changing technology.

- Consumerism for new products and new services.
- Concern for total quality control and cost effectiveness.
- Internationalization of social costs due to industrialization.
- Customer satisfaction and fulfillment of psycho–emotional needs of customers.
- Employ empowerment.

Globalization has emerged in the realm of business in recent years. It is an important matter in all business conferences all over the world.

Now, globalization has attained a very important place in the business environment. For example, Japan has achieved a spectacular success through its global approach to business. Companies are now trying to establish their corporate identity as corporate citizens.

In this century it has become necessary to adopt corporate strategies to operate in global business environment for all business organizations. Consequently, every organization must have a global approach in business whether it is for local or regional or world market.

4. Nature of Globalization

Most thinkers consider globalization as international multinational or transnational. Levitt called it as "Globalization of market". Though globalization of business may include all of those, but it is matter of these.

Globalization of business is a state of mind viewing one's business in a global perspective. It requires global outlook, globally viable technology and maintaining global quality standards so that it can offer the products and services satisfying the customers' needs in a global environment. Further, it should maintain global quality standards, global corporate identity and a global business culture.

Thus, globalization requires an integration of various countries with different economic systems with each other.

The world trade agreements and formation of economic blocks have provided ample scope for the companies to operate throughout the world.

Globalization of business has a world-wide approach as the entire world is viewed as one entity, one people and one market.

The recent trend all over the globe reveals a move for privatization backed by environmental complexities, large scale operation, dynamic technological development, operation of market forces, homogeneity in demand and supply, which have subsquently encouraged globalization.

Thus, a global business and market philosophy has been fast emerging. Most countries are trying to integrate themselves with the global business for which control and regulatory measures were relaxed and privatization introduced in a big way.

India, too, is also following the policy of privatization not only to keep herself integrated with the rest of the world, but also to maintain economic viability of business organizations.

The recent political and economic changes in the socialist and communist countries together with liberalization of multilateral trade and investment have compelled them to adopt globalization of business.

Now-a-days, companies are becoming more globalized in their production, marketing and other functions. For example Toyota, Japan's second largest automobile company in the world has its more than two-third of business outside Japan.

Thus, a global corporation considers the entire world as a single market. It does not distinguish between domestic and foreign markets, but considers only one global market.

Hence, the raw materials, components, machinery,

technology and finances etc. are obtained from the cheapest source from any part of the world.

Further, product development and production planning are considered on the basis of global market.

More and more companies are adopting such a global strategic orientation. In India, it has been taken by Arvind Mills. A company has to pass through various stages before it adopts globalization

5. Cross Border Transfer of Knowledge

In line with rapid globalization of economic activity, cross-border transactions by corporations have exploded over the last 20 years.

With this huge increase in the cross-border business, the need for effective cross-border knowledge transfer is greater than ever and will continue to increase. Understanding international knowledge transfer is not only increasingly crucial to the success of multinational corporations, it is also critical to transferring any work related knowledge.

6. National Culture and Cultural Distance Shape the Perceived Value of Knowledge

Research has shown that the greater the cultural differences, the more difficulties people have in receiving unit in seeing the advantages of adopting knowledge or organization practices from the source unit.

Even if employees in the receiving unit see the value in adopting certain routines and practices from the source unit, the perceived and often real cost involved in doing so are likely to be higher when countries are culturally distant.

Differences in cognitive structures, values and practices as well as languages and communication barriers, all raise the costs involved in knowledge transfer; as a result the parties involved in the knowledge transfer are less likely to share and apply new knowledge.

7. National Culture and Cultural Differences Shape the Motivational Disposition of the Source Unit

Transferring knowledge is not cost free. It is also very much context bound. Managers and employees as source unit must spend time and resources to provide relevant knowledge to the target unit. Their willingness to do this is likely to be affected by their own national culture.

Two different types of cultures collectivism, institutional and in-group collectivist, are likely to have opposite effects on the source unit's motivation to transfer knowledge. Managers in a high in-group collectivist culture are used to working closely with the members of in-group but are less concerned with knowledge transfer and those outside their group. They are reluctant to spend the time and the effort to build close relationship with outsider. In contrast, manger from a high institutional collectivist culture tends to promote and encourage more system – wide information system and knowledge transfer to encourage greater organization – wide communication and collaboration.

8. Cultural Differences Affect Richness to Transmission Channels and create Communication Barriers

Any form of knowledge transfer requires substantial high quality communication between the parties. In cross – border cases, this is most important and hard to achieve. The most basic barrier is language. Even though English is the predominant language of cross-border communications, managers in many parts of the world do not have a good command of English. This can cause communications problem, especially in cases of non-face to face communication.

One way to deal with such problems is to increase the level of face-to-face contact. However, this is relatively time consuming and expensive in most cross-border settings.

Another important issue related to communication is the methods used by the source unit to transfer knowledge.

Differences in cultural practice can play an important role here. When the transfer is from high uncertainty avoidance culture and the receiving unit is from a low uncertainty culture, the parties may find the knowledge transfer process frustrating. This is because the former will rephrase organized, formal and structured forms of communication, while the latter will prefer informal, unplanned and unstructured approaches.

9. National Culture and Cultural Differences shape the Motivational Disposition and Absorptive Capacity of the Target Unit

Research on knowledge transfer has shown that a target unit's absorption of new knowledge depends in part on its stock of prior related knowledge.

Knowledge development is path-dependent and cumulative in a shape that it consists of a gradual and in mental process of learning; the new knowledge gets connected to the existing related knowledge and builds on it.

Totally new knowledge has no anchor in organizational memory. Therefore, it cannot book into an existing piece of knowledge.

Existing knowledge can thus enhance the target units ability and motivation to better understand and evaluate the new incoming knowledge.

A unit faced with totally new knowledge may therefore be unable to determine its relevance and value. The inability to assess the value of the in coming knowledge, in turn reduces the motivation and ability of the target firm to invest the energy and effort to assimilate and exploit it.

A target unit's absorptive capacity is also affected by the cultural difference between the source and target unit. The degree of similarity between both units, in terms of values and beliefs (among other things) is important. This is because when individuals or groups share common meanings, they find it easier to communicate, and the target unit is more receptive to the new knowledge.

10. How to Manage Cross Culture Issues

Now we suggest as to how managers can better manage the transfer of knowledge across cultures.

10.1 Define Common Goals in Advance to Knowledge Transfer

Fore most, it is important for parties involved in knowledge transfer to agree on a set of common goals and objectives in their joint initiative.

Criteria for defining success need to be identified by parties and agreed to in advance. This is critical because we know that culturally different parties define success differently and, as a result, expect different goals and attach different values to prospective knowledge transfer.

If parties agree, they are more likely to converge on how important the knowledge is and what to expect from the process.

An important element in defining common goals is the perceived value of the knowledge content.

It is important that the parties understand and agree on the value and applicability of the knowledge to be transferred before they agree on their common goals.

A critical success factor in a cross-boarder knowledge transfer is an agreement on how and why the particular knowledge is of value to the target unit. Such a discussion will result in a better understanding of the target unit's needs and may lead to change in the content of the knowledge to be transferred

10.2 Map the Cultural Profiles

Parties involved in cross-border knowledge transfer must understand their own and the other side's cultural profiles.

The profiles enable an understanding of how they are

different or similar on that basis. Key members of the parties to the transfer should engage in a discussion of the different cultures. It is advised to do so very early on in the transfer process.

The parties need to identify the subset of cultural differences that can negatively impact the process and explore possible ways to address them. As such early in process can be helpful and contexture, it prevents an emotional or confrontational debate and facilitates a rational, preemptive and constructive approach. Discussion on cultural profiles should not be only focused on cultural differences.

A review of the specific cross-cultural similarities can help put the parties at ease. It can identify potential areas of leverage to help deal with the cultural differences and possible areas of convergences are similar cultural values.

10.3 Assign Relationship to Managers in Cross Cultural Transfer of Knowledge

The parties involved in cross-border knowledge need more than open lines of communications. They need to create a common space where the party feel comfortable and confident to work together as well as create and develop the mutual relationship.

The common space is developed through an understanding of common cultural traits and common goals for the transfer, but it also requires constant contacts, in the form of both distant and pace to pace and formal and social exchanges to develop the requisite trust. Especially in the case of a high in-group culture, the challenges for the external partner is to find ways that would help it become part of the other parties in – group social and informal gathering tend to the particularly important in such settings.

10.4 Learn from Knowledge Transfer

The parties involved in cross-cultural knowledge transfer

need to see it as a learning opportunity The success of organization is increasingly dependent on productive relationship with people in other culturally different organization. Cross-cultural knowledge transfer is a fact of daily life for most corporations worldwide. It is therefore desirable for manager to view each case of knowledge transfer not as an isolated situation but as a point in a steam of learning opportunity. Time and money need to be brigaded and spent on this cross-cultural learning.

11. Concluding Remarks

In this paper we have discussed the issues related to cross-border transfer of knowledge. The essence of our article is that while any case of knowledge transfer may face obstacles and complexities, cases of cross-borders knowledge transfer may face an extra challenge of cross-cultural hurdles.

But cultural differences do not per secreate problems; rather it is the way that cultural differences are managed and that often results in poor knowledge transfer outcomes.

If managed effectively, cultural differences can be a source of synergy and a stimulus for mutual learning. They need to be aware of how the partnering cultures are different and be mindful of their implications.

As explained in the paper, the parties need to define their common goals in the transfer and their success criteria, need to understand and discuss their potential cultural challenges, need to ensure they have proper management of the relationship and need to treat every case of cross-border knowledge transfer as a learning opportunity to improve their chances for next time.

****

12

Globalization: Conceptual Framework and Transition

*Priyanka Kapoor**

Globalization has different meaning for different people. Many view it as an economic phenomenon, involving the increasing interaction, or integration, of national economic systems through the growth in international trade, investment and capital flows. Some view it as a rapid increase in cross-border social, cultural and technological exchange. The sociologist, Anthony Giddens, defines globalization as a decoupling of space and time, emphasizing that with instantaneous communications, knowledge and culture can be shared around the world simultaneously. Ruud Lubbers defines it as a process in which geographic distance becomes a factor of diminishing importance in the establishment and maintenance of cross border economic, political and socio-cultural relations. Left critics of Globalization define the word quite differently, presenting it as worldwide drive toward a globalized economic system dominated by supranational corporate trade and banking institutions that are not accountable to democratic processes or national governments. David Held and Anthony McGrew wrote in their entry for Oxford Companion to Politics that globalization can be conceived as a process (or set of processes) which embodies a transformation in the spatial

* Research Scholar, Department of Sociology, R.G. Post-graduate College (CCS University), Meerut (India)

organization of social relations and transactions, expressed in transcontinental or interregional flows and networks of activity, interaction and power.

1. Different Connotations of Globalization

Globalization is an undeniably capitalist process. It has taken off as a concept in the wake of the collapse of the Soviet Union and of socialism as a viable alternate form of economic organization. "Globalization" can have any of the following connotation according to the perception of the person looking at it:

1. Globalism, if the concept is reduced to its economic aspects, can be said to contrast with economic nationalism and protectionism. It is related to laissez-faire capitalism and neoliberalism.
2. It shares a number of characteristics with internationalization and is often used interchangeably, although some prefer to use globalization to emphasize the erosion of the nation-state or national boundaries.
3. Making connections between places on a global scale. Today, more and more places around the world are connected to each other in ways that were previously unimaginable. In Geography, this process is known as complex connectivity, where more and more places are being connected in more and more ways. Arjun Appadurai identified five types of global connectivity :
    i. Ethnoscapes : movements of people, including tourists, immigrants, refugees, and business travellers.
    ii. Financescapes : global flows of money, often driven by interconnected currency markets, stock exchanges, and commodity markets.
    iii. Ideoscapes : the global spread of ideas and political ideologies.

iv. Mediascapes : the global distribution of media images that appear on our computer screens, in newspapers, television, and radio.

v) Technoscapes : the movement of technologies around the globe.

Although Appadurai's taxonomy is highly contestable, it does serve to show that globalization is much more than economics on a global scale. Practically globalization refers to:

1. In its cultural form, globalization has been a label used to identify attempts to erode the national cultures of Europe, and subsume them into a global culture whose members will be much easier to manipulate through mass media and controlled governments.

2. The formation of a global village – closer contact between different parts of the world, with increasing possibilities of personal exchange, mutual understanding and friendship between "world citizens", and creation of a global civilization.

3. Economic globalization – there are four aspects to economic globalization, referring to four different flows across boundaries, namely flows of goods/services, i.e. 'free trade' (or at least freer trade), flows of people (migration), of capital, and of technology. A consequence of economic globalization is increasing relations among members of an industry in different parts of the world (globalization of an industry), with a corresponding erosion of National Sovereignty in the economic sphere. The IMF defines globalization as "the growing economic interdependence of countries worldwide through increasing volume and variety of cross-border transactions in goods and services, freer international capital flows, and more rapid and widespread diffusion of technology" (IMF, *World Economic*

Outlook, May, 1997). The World Bank defines globalization as the "Freedom and ability of individuals and firms to initiate voluntary economic transactions with residents of other countries".

4. In the field of Management, globalization is a Marketing or Strategy term that refers to the emergence of international markets for consumer goods characterized by similar customer needs and tastes enabling, for example, selling the same cars or soaps or foods with similar ad campaigns to people in different cultures. This usage is contrasted with internationalization which describes the activities of multinational companies dealing across borders in either financial instruments, commodities, or products that are extensively tailored to local markets. Globalization also means cross-border management activities or development processes to adapt to the emergence of a globalized market or to seek and realize benefit from economies of scale or scope or from cross-border learning among different country-based organizations.
5. In the field of software, globalization is a technical term that combines the development processes of internationalization and localization.
6. For anti-captalist groups such as socialists and communists, globalization is a catch-all term for the alleged negative effects of for-profit multinational corporations and the use of legal and financial means to circumvent local laws and standards, in order to leverage the labor and services of unequally-developed regions against each other.
7. The spread of capitalism from developed to developing nations.
8. "The concept of Globalization refers both to the compression of the world and the intensification of consciousness of the world as a whole".

2. History of Globalization

There is no agreed answer to when did globalization began. But understanding of globalization is helped by understanding a brief history of globalization. Since the word has both technical and political meanings, different groups will have differing histories of "globalization". In general use within the field of economics and political economy, however, it is a history of increasing trade between nations based on stable institutions that allow firms in different nations to exchange goods with minimal friction.

The term "liberalization" came to mean the combination of laissez-faire economic theory with the removal of barriers to the movement of goods. This led to specialization of nations in exports, and the pressure to end protective tariffs and other barriers to trade. The period of the gold standard and liberalization of the 19th century is often called "The First Era of Globalization". Based on the Pax Britannica and the exchange of goods in currencies pegged to specie, this era grew along with industrialization. The theoretical basis was David Ricardo's work on Comparative advantage and Say's Law of General equilibrium. In essence, it was argued that nations would trade effectively, and that any temporary disruptions in supply or demand would correct themselves automatically. The institution of the gold standard came in steps in major industrialized nations between approximately 1850 and 1880, though exactly when various nations were truly on the gold standard is contentiously debated.

The "First Era of Globalization" is said to have broken down in stages beginning with the First World War, and then collapsing with the crisis of the gold standard in the late 1920's and early 1930's. Countries that engaged in that era of globalization, including the European core, some of the European periphery and various European offshoots in the Americas and Oceania, prospered. Inequality between those states fell, as goods, capital and labour flowed remarkably freely between nations.

Globalization in the era since World War II has been driven by Trade Negotiation Rounds, originally under the auspices of GATT, which led to a series of agreements to remove restrictions on "free trade". The Uruguay round led to a treaty to create the World Trade Organization or WTO, to mediate trade disputes. Other bilateral trade agreements, including sections of Europe's Maastricht Treaty and the North American Free Trade Agreement have also been signed in pursuit of the goal of reducing tariffs and barriers to trade. In India the process of globalization and liberalization started from 1991.

3. Players of Globalization

The major players of globalization are :

1. *The World Trade Organization (WTO)* was established in 1995 to administer the rules of international trade agreed to by its 123 member countries. These rules have been ratified by the parliaments of all members. The key difference between the WTO and the General Agreement on Tariffs and Trade (GATT), which it replaced, is that the WTO is a permanent organization with the judicial powers to rule on international trade disputes. The WTO also covers trade in services, whereas GATT only covered trade in goods. The WTO's rules make it hard for a country to favour their own industry over imports from other countries. Also, the WTO rules do not allow a country to favour the imports of one country over those from another. The WTO argues that the growth of trade between countries increases the wealth of everyone. Trade allows the production of goods and services by those who are most efficient, thus maximizing their availability at the best price.The growth of trade is helped by the lowering of barriers, such as tariffs and import quotas, which is the object of WTO agreements.

2. ***The International Monetary Fund (IMF)*** was established in the wake of the World War II in 1946 to:

   i) Promote international cooperation on finance,

   ii) Encourage stability in exchange rates and orderly systems for exchanging money between countries

   iii) Providing temporary assistance for countries suffering balance of payments problems

The IMF frequently seeks institutional reform in the countries to which it provides temporary financial assistance. Like the WTO, the IMF believes that world prosperity is enhanced by greater exchange between nations and that this is made possible by everyone agreeing to abide by rules. The IMF has 182 member countries.

3. The *World Bank* provides loans to poor countries for development projects. The bank provides loans for investment projects, such as water and sanitation, natural resource management education and health. It also lends for what it calls adjustment projects, which are to support governments undertaking policy reforms, such as improved public sector management.

4. Established at the conclusion of the World War II, the United Nations has become a promoter of globalization, arguing that individual states have a dual role with responsibilities to both their own citizens and to the world society as a whole. The United Nations says the broader global responsibility requires international institutions. It supports the case for reform of international institutions, including its own Security Council, to make them more representative. The UN has sponsored a Global Compact to establish and promote a shared set of core values in the areas of labour standards, human rights and environmental practices between the UN and the business community.

5. *The Organization for Economic Cooperation and Development (OECD)* develops economic and social policy for its 29 members, which include the countries of North America, Western Europe (including Czech Republic, Hungary and Poland) and Japan, Korea, Australia and New Zealand. It provides economic arguments for globalization, such as data demonstrating the positive contribution made by multinational corporations to economic development.
6. ***United Nations Conference on Trade and Development (UNCTAD)*** is a permanent intergovernmental body of the UN that aims to maximize the trade investment and development opportunities of developing economies and to assist their efforts to integrate into the world economy.
7. The ***World Economic Forum (WEF)*** is a private not-for-profit foundation that operates conferences for business, political, intellectual and other society leaders. The WEF holds an annual conference in the Swiss town of Davos, where it is based, and also holds regional conferences around the world. It has no decision-making power, but many of the world's business and political leaders discuss issues of importance at WEF meetings.
8. ***Public Affairs Organizations:*** *World growth organization* is dedicated to providing a balance to the debate about trade, globalization and sustainable development. It focuses on market based approaches to trade and growth for securing benefits in both developed and developing countries. The *Institute of Economic Affairs* is a UK based free market think tank that aims to explain free market ideas including the benefits of globalization. *International Policy Network* (IPN) and the Competitive Enterprise Institute (CEI) are non-profit, non government organizations that research and share ideas and issues such as globalization, global warming, sustainable development and intellectual property.

9. ***Businesses Benefiting from Open International Markets:*** Most organizations representing business endorse globalization and efforts to lower barriers to international trade and investment. For example, the International Chamber of Commerce argues that economic growth is essential if living standards around the world are to increase. Economic growth, it argues, is generated by trade. Another international business organization, the World Business Council for Sustainable Development is working to build support for the UN's "Global Compact".

10. ***Developing country governments and NGOs perceiving benefit from open markets:*** Most of the world's governments and parliaments are signatories to the World Trade Organization, and members of the International Monetary Fund. A number of the richer nations among the developing world, such as Mexico, Turkey, Egypt and Thailand, have provided vocal support for globalization.

11. ***Internet and telecommunications industry:*** One of the driving forces of globalization is the advance of telecommunications in general and the internet in particular. Representative organizations regard the spread of communications technology as a benefit without qualification. For example, the International Telecommunications Union sees globalization as the innate human desire for the integration of individuals in villages and cities and the integration of people of all races and backgrounds into nations. Other organizations are concerned that the free spread of communications technology proceeds without impediment of censorship or any other official constraint. See for example the Global Internet Liberty Campaign.

12. ***Left critics of capitalism:*** The *World Social Forum* emerged as a counterpoint to the World Economic Forum. It represents a broad range of interests and civil society groups

with the ambitious aim of rebuilding the dreams of the left in today's globalized world. Marxist organizations see globalization as the spread of capitalism, in which the labour of the poor is exploited for the benefit of the rich. Leftist Parties of the World is an excellent directory.Left organizations have mounted the series of "global action days" starting with the WTO summit in Seattle in September 1999, and targeting meetings of the World Bank, the IMF and the private business conference organization, the World Economic Forum. Websites are established around each of these action days, for example the Genoa Social Forum demonstration against the G-8 meeting held in July 2001 where Carlo Guiliani died during protests.

13. ***Business Organizations Threatened by International Competition:*** Many companies in rich countries oppose globalization because they fear that competition from imports will cost them money. Such companies are typically found in industries such as textiles and footwear. These are among the few industries in which poor countries can provide effective competition. Many business organizations that may support the world trade system in general will oppose specific measures to reduce tariffs, which is one of the principal means for building global trade.

14. ***Unions in Rich Countries :*** Some trade unions oppose globalization, saying that it leads to a lowering of wage and workplace standards. The argument generally presented is that globalization encourages the trade in goods produced in countries which do not allow unions to defend their workers' rights. They undercut the goods produced in countries where unions do defend unions' rights. This leads to a 'race to the bottom' as the markets are won by those with the lowest standards. Not all unions take this stand. Globalization does not figure among the Australian Council of Trade Unions campaigns, but is a

matter of importance for the American Union movement, the AFL-CIO As with businesses, the most vocal unions on globalization issues tends to be those representing workers in industries in which there are strong competitors in developing countries. In Australia, the Australian Manufacturing Workers Union, led by Doug Cameron, has made the strongest campaign for 'fair trade', as opposed to 'free trade'.

15. ***Cultural nationalists:*** Some regard globalization as the spread of American culture and influence. It is also often expressed in France, leading, for example, to the assault on a McDonalds Store by a farm leader, Jose Bove, who provided milk for French Roquefort Cheese.

4. Nature and Existence of Globalization

There is much academic discussion about whether globalization is a real phenomenon or only an analytical artifact (a myth). Although the term is widespread, many authors argue that the characteristics attributed to globalization have already been seen at other moments in history. Also, many note that such features, including the increase in international trade and the greater role of multinational corporations, are not as deeply established as they may appear. Thus, many authors prefer the term internationalization rather than globalization. In internationalization, the role of the state and the importance of nations are greater, while globalization in its complete form eliminates nation states. So, they argue that the frontiers of countries, in a broad sense, are far from being dissolved, and therefore this radical globalization process is not happening, and probably will not happen considering that in world history, internationalization never turned into globalization.

However, the world increasingly shares problems and challenges that do not obey nation-state borders, most notably pollution of the natural environment, and the movement previously known as anti-globalization has transformed into a movement of movements for globalization from below, seeking, through experimentation, forms of social organization that transcend the nation-state and representative democracy. Whereas the original arguments that globalization is taking place can be refuted with stories of internationalisation, as above, the emergence of a global movement is indisputable and therefore we can speak of a real process towards a global human society of societies. Other authors have argued that we are in transition to a planetary phase of civilization; the exact form and character of the global society is contested and will be determined by the choices we make in the critical decades ahead.

5. Characteristics of Globalization

Globalization has become identified with a number of trends, most of which may have developed since World War II. These include greater international movement of commodities, money, information, and people; and the development of technology, organizations, legal systems, and infrastructures to allow this movement. The actual existence of some of these trends is as under which can be classified as different characteristics of globalization.

1. Economically
   - i) Increase in international trade at a faster rate than the growth in the world economy.
   - ii) Increase in international flow of capital including foreign direct investment.
   - iii) Erosion of national sovereignty and national borders through international agreements leading to organizations like the WTO and OPEC.
   - iv) Development of global financial systems
   - v) Increase in the share of the world economy controlled by multinational corporations.
   - vi) Increased role of international organizations such as

WTO, WIPO, IMF that deal with international transactions.

vii) Increase of economic practices like outsourcing, by multinational corporations.

2. Culturally

   i) Greater international cultural exchange.

   ii) Spreading of multiculturalism, and better individual access to cultural diversity, for example through the export of Hollywood and Bollywood movies. However, the imported culture can easily supplant the local culture, causing reduction in diversity through hybridization or even assimilation. The most prominent form of this is Westernization, but Sinicization of cultures also takes place.

   iii) Greater international travel and tourism.

   iv) Greater immigration, including illegal immigration.

   v) Spread of local foods such as pizza and Indian food to other countries (often adapted to local taste).

3. Development of a global telecommunications infrastructure and greater transborder data flow, using such technologies as the Internet, communication satellites and telephones.

4. Increases in the number of standards applied globally; e.g. copyright laws and patents.

5. Formation or development of a set of universal values.

6. The push by many advocates for an international criminal court and international justice movements (see the International Criminal Court and International Court of Justice respectively).

7. Some argue that even terrorism has undergone globalization, with attacks in foreign countries that have no direct relation with the own country.

8. Promotion of free trade

   i) Of goods:

      a. Reduction or elimination of tariffs; construction of free trade zones with small or no tariffs.

      b. Reduced transportation costs, especially from development of containerization for ocean shipping.

   ii) Of capital : reduction or elimination of capital controls.

   iii) Reduction, elimination, or harmonization of subsidies for local businesses.

9. **Intellectual Property Restrictions**

   i) Harmonization of intellectual property laws across nations (generally speaking, with more restrictions).

   ii) Supranational recognition of intellectual property restrictions (e.g. patents granted by China would be recognized in the US).

6. Globalization

A term coined by Roland Robertson, glocalization describes a process whereby the "local" is integrated into the "global". This results in a heterigenization of cultures, as local quiditties of particular areas become disseminated around the world, and cultures clash with newly introduced cultural concepts, ideologies, practices, and so on. One keen example of glocalization is that of museums. Museums take local culture and history and prepare them for mass consumption, especially among tourists. Such manufacturing of local culture for mass consumption results in heterogenization, rather than homogenization, because it introduces, rather than supplants, the local culture.

Globalization is an opposing theory to that of "Grobalization", a term coined by George Ritzer to identify globalization with cultural homogenization. Here, the manufacturing of cultural artifacts is taken to involve the *homogenization* of such artifacts, so as to be apt to be consumed by many consumers around the world.

Within the contemporary debate about globalization, the debate regarding *globalization*-versus-*grobalization* is widespread. There have been major proponents of both, and each theory carries with it its own set of differing interpretations. For example, Appadurai is a proponent of a theory of *hybridization*, which may be associated with globalization, whereby there is occurring an overall heterogenization of cultures, and a creation of new cultures resulting from clashes among various *-scapes*.

While the dispute has yet to be fully reconciled, each theory carries with it it's own pros and cons. Furthermore, it is certain that globalization cannot be viewed as a unidimensional phenomenon. Indeed, the study of globalization carries multiple theories, especially with respect to the cultural dimensions of globalization, regarding the characteristics, and entailed processes, contained within the contemporary process of globalization.

7. Anti-globalization

Various aspects of globalization are seen as harmful by public-interest activists as well as strong state nationalists. This movement has no unified name. "Anti-globalization" is the media's preferred term; it can lead to some confusion, as activists typically oppose certain aspects or forms of globalization, not globalization per se. Indeed, the global justice movement is a common name. Many activists also unite under the slogan "another world is possible", which has given rise to names such as *altermondialisme* in French.

There is a wide variety of kinds of "anti-globalization". In general, critics claim that the results of globalization have not been what was predicted when the attempt to increase free trade began, and that many institutions involved in the system of globalization have not taken the interests of poorer nations and the working class into account.

Economic arguments by fair trade theorists claim that unrestricted free trade benefits those with more financial leverage (i.e. the rich) at the expense of the poor. Many "anti-globalization" activists see globalization as the promotion of a corporatist agenda, which is intent on constricting the freedoms of individuals in the name of profit. They also claim that increasing autonomy and strength of corporate entities increasingly shape the political policy of nation-states. Some "anti-globalization" groups argue that globalization is necessarily imperialistic, is one of the driving reasons behind the Iraq war and that it has forced savings to flow into the United States rather than developing nations. Some argue that globalization imposes credit-based economics, resulting in *unsustainable* growth of debt and debt crises. The main opposition is to *unfettered* globalization (neoliberal; laissez-faire capitalism), guided by governments and what are claimed to be quasi-governments (such as the International Monetary Fund and the World Bank) that are supposedly not held responsible to the populations that they govern and instead respond mostly to the interests of corporations. Many conferences between trade and finance ministers of the core globalizing nations have been met with large, and occasionally violent, protests from opponents of "corporate globalism".

Some "anti-globalization" activists object to the fact that the current "globalization" globalizes money and corporations, but not people and unions. This can be seen in the strict immigration controls in nearly all countries, and the lack of labour rights in many countries in the developing world. Another more conservative camp opposed to globalization are state-centric nationalists who fear globalization is displacing the role of nations in global politics and point to NGOs as impeding upon the power of individual nations.

The movement is very broad, including church groups, national liberation factions, left-wing parties, environmentalists, peasant unionists, anti-racism groups, libertarian socialists, and others. Most are reformist (arguing for a more humane form of capitalism) and a strong minority is revolutionary (arguing for a more humane system than capitalism). Many have decried the lack of unity and direction in the movement, but some have claimed that this lack of centralization may in fact be a strength.

Protests by the global justice movement have forced high-level international meetings away from the major cities where they used to be held, into remote locations where protest is impractical.

8. Pro-globalization (Globalism)

Supporters of democratic globalization can be labelled pro-globalists. They consider that the first phase of globalization, which was market-oriented, should be completed by a phase of building global political institutions representing the will of World citizens. The difference with other globalists is that they do not define in advance any ideology to orient this will, which should be left to the free choice of those citizens via a democratic process.

Supporters of free trade point out that economic theories of comparative advantage suggest that free trade leads to a more efficient allocation of resources, with all countries involved in the trade benefiting. In general, they claim that this leads to lower prices, more employment and higher output.

Libertarians and other proponents of laissez-faire capitalism say higher degrees of political and economic freedom in the form of democracy and capitalism in the developed world produce higher levels of material wealth. They see globalization as the beneficial spread of liberty and capitalism.

Critics argue that the anti-globalization movement uses anecdotal evidence to support their view and that worldwide statistics instead strongly support globalization:

1. The percentage of people in developing countries living below US$1 (adjusted for inflation and purchasing power) per day has halved in only twenty years, although some critics argue that more detailed variables measuring poverty should instead be studied.
2. Life expectancy has almost doubled in the developing world since WWII and is starting to close the gap to the developed world where the improvement has been smaller. Child mortality has decreased in every developing region of the world. Income inequality for the world as a whole is diminishing
3. Democracy has increased dramatically from almost no nation with universal suffrage
4. The proportion of the world's population living in countries where per-capita food supplies are under 2,200 calories (9,200 kilojoules) per day decreased from 56 percent in the mid-1960s to below 10 percent by the 1990s.
5. Between 1950 and 1999, global literacy increased from 52 percent to 81 percent of the world. Women made up much of the gap: Female literacy as a percentage of male literacy has increased from 59 percent in 1970 to 80 percent in 2000.
6. There are similar trends for electric power, cars, radios, and telephones per capita, as well as the proportion of the population with access to clean water

However, some of these improvements may not be due to globalization, or may be possible without the current form of globalization or its negative consequences, to which the global justice movement objects. Many pro-capitalists are also critical of the World Bank and the IMF, arguing that they are corrupt bureaucracies controlled and financed by states, not corporations. Many loans have been given to dictators who never carried out promised reforms, instead leaving the common people to pay the debts later. They thus see too little capitalism, not too much. They also note that some of the resistance to globalization comes from special interest groups with conflicting interests, like Western world unions.

Others, simply view globalization as inevitable and advocate creating institutions such as a directly-elected United Nations Parliamentary Assembly to exercise oversight over unelected international bodies.

9. The Transition to Global Society

There have been transitions in the past. But now when we are in the 21st century, we are involved in the most crucial and most difficult of all the transitions so far, *the transition to the global society.* It now becomes clear that, impelled by science and technology, all aspects of our life on this planet are undergoing a process of globalization and constant change.

In economics, commerce, in trade, in industry decisions are no longer confined to individual nations. As the market economy dominates the economic scene on this planet, we find that economics and commerce are far exceeding and transcending national barriers. Economics and commerce are rapidly becoming global.

The environment is global. It is universally accepted that the environment and environmental problems are no longer susceptible to solutions by nation states. Whether it is the attention of the ozone layer, or deforestation, the pollution of rivers and oceans or disappearance of wild life, or the pollution of air, water, food, everything that is happening is *now* of global dimension.

Communication par excellence has been most dramatic manifestation of globalization. The breaking of the space barrier, satellite technology, the development of television and telecommunication, electronic mail, superhighway information technology, internet interaction is potent forces of globalization. Television enables us to become global citizens by simply sitting in our rooms. Never before has it been possible for crores of people to concentrate their attention on one single event

(TV/Video) at a single moment of time, and the effect that this will have on the culture of succeeding generation is still impossible to quantify. Whether we like it or not, we are global citizens now, thanks largely to televisions, computers and global telecommunications.

There are only two languages today that of computer Mathematics and English. In music, young people are dancing and singing to the same rhythms, whether it is New York, Delhi, Singapore, Beijing, Mumbai, London, Paris, Moscow or Tokyo. It is the heart-throb of a new global civilization that we are hearing. Dress, fashion, food, brands, drinks one can go on developing the global theme. In short, we are in an unprecedented and irrevocable process of globalization which is strongly influencing all the peoples of the world, whether they like it or not, for the better or for the worse. A new kind of civilization we are witnessing.

Business organization in a country no longer can afford to remain competitive only in the national market. It has to acquire competitiveness now in the global market and aspire to increase its market share in the global market. No longer is the U.S.A. enjoying virtual monopoly in the automobile market even within the U.S.A. (*i.e.,* home country). The labour cost in the U.S.A. is quite high. Production facilities in other countries are relatively low cheaper. U.S. automobile was priced out in the home country. We have now contest among nations in the global market.

Unparalleled developments have started happening and again what has happened is that the time has *telescoped* most of the radical changes brought about by globalization has taken place in our own lifetime, e.g., Jet aviation. In jetliners, within a few hours you are at the other end of the world. Live telecasting enables you to see and enjoy any programme all over the world as it is taking place in any country. TV has literally become an integral part of the people's consciousness everywhere. Breaking of the space barrier and landing on the moon happened in our own lifetimes. Computerization, robotics, organ transplant, genetic engineering – all these mind-boggling developments have taken place just in the course of forty years. This is a very strange and disturbing situation.

One important factor is non-emergence of global consciousness on the one hand there is the rapid emergence of the global society, and on the other, our mind-set is still largely mired in preglobal concepts and perceptions, because we have been brought up in a different kind of world. Even today our educational systems are hardly adjusted to the new situation. Therefore, there is a time lag; there is this tension that is developing between the emergence of global society and the non-emergence of global consciousness.

Many of the ills from which we suffer today, *e.g.,* widespread terrorism, violence, individual and collective, widespread poverty, malnutrition, widespread corruption, AIDS (spreading over a wide area) etc., can be traced to the tardy emergence of a global consciousness to sustain global society that has now developed. How do we *bridge* this gap? What is it that needs to be done?

10. Conclusion

"The Third Millennium will be *ethical* and *spiritual or* there will be no third millennium." Atomic- energy can be a boon or a curse in the world. Unless the world has an ethical and spiritual *rebirth,* we would not realize Global Ethicality, Spirituality, and Global Soul.

A human being in the Global Society must have four values or virtues. Intellectual virtues or qualities are more important than physical qualities. Moral and ethical values have greater significance than intellectual qualities. Spiritual values are of paramount importance than even ethical values. Moral qualities like love and affection, compassion and understanding, tolerance, the attitude of *'live and let live'* and spiritual virtues like faith in one self, the purity of one's inner oneness, unity in humanity, Nature and Earth are the real expressions of *global consciousness,* global society envisaged in the impending third millennium starting from 2001 AD. The global society would then be a holy family of nations. May we cherish the realization of this sweet dream when we enter into the *third millennium!*

We seek to emphasize the *wholeness* or *oneness* of the universe and oneness of life in plants, animals, and human beings. With the scientific and technological advancement of the current century, the world has become a global village and all citizens of the world have to contribute their mite to ensure that the *Planet Earth* is saved from the ongoing scars and corruptions and perdition in various spheres of human life.

For this purpose Ecology and human character have to work together and develop new paradigms for harmony, balance or equilibrium with Nature so that humanity, plants, and animals can live in harmony with each other and evolve the Planet Earth as a place with Peace and Pleasure. Unless we develop the spirit and consciousness of a global family among humans cannot survive in the third millennium because of various crises like ecological degradation, unrestrained consumerism, unnatural life-style, social disintegration, and decadence in ethical, moral and spiritual values of life, inner disharmony, in addition to the ongoing scars of Conflict, War, Terrorism on the one hand, poverty, over-population, inner/outer pollution, on the other.

Holism and global consciousness are required. Holism expresses Unity of God, Nature, and Individuals. We have One Father. All of us are his children. He is not far. He is not near. He is within our heart chambers. He is, indeed, with us. We can never be alone or lonely.

His Spirit pervades all beings. He is the Creator, Preserver and Destroyer. He is always moved by Love and Compassion. He kindles in every heart. God's Love is comparable with the love of a mother embracing her child in the intensity of love.

His mercy is inexhaustible. He is limitless, infinite. He is the Saviour. He saves us from all sins. We can commune with him only in absolute silence.

What is required is the emergence of global consciousness. The key to the emergence of global consciousness lies in the meeting of science and spirituality, in the running of these two great disciplines. Science is the search for truth going outwards into the heart of *matter,* and the spirituality is the search of truth, going inwards into the heart chamber *within* us. But they have diverged. We must adopt value-driven holistic approach and seek convergence or reunion between matter and spirit, the two great inputs. Then only we will evolve *enduring* global consciousness and achieve glorious human civilization. We will then have both external and internal prosperity, higher standard of life (quality of life) and quantity of life, *i.e.,* standard of living in our global society. We must expand and widen our consciousness to establish global union.

The great achievements of science/technology need not be denied, whether in medicine or in surgery, in communications or in raising living standards. But today there is a great *poison* also not only in the outer pollution of the planet but even more dangerously in the inner pollution that is taking place in our mind and heart *e.g.,* the hatreds, jealousies, animosities, crisis of values. Friends, we must realize that we are standing at a *cross road* which road will we take? One road will take us to harmony, happiness and all round prosperity. The other road to disaster, destruction, decay and death of our civilization. This is stark reality. .

Are we going to continue on the road of hatred, conflict and stupid competition? Or are we going to take the other road which has been *less used* so far - the road of harmony, integration, co-operation and teamwork?

Let us have the *shreyas* road, the road of human and ethical values, and the road of holism rather than the disjointed and fragmented consciousness in which the human race is at present involved. This is the *challenge* before us, before *each one of us.* The choice is yours. Let us not miss a unique opportunity. Let us develop global consciousness to enjoy the sweet fruits of global society.

Each one of us in our own life has got to develop this global consciousness. We have to remember that while we are individuals, the individual has the divine spark in him/her. We are also part of the *extended* human family *(global family).* Hence, we have two goals in our life. We work for the salvation of our own souls and also for the welfare of the society.

"0 Lord, you are the cause of all causes. Wisdom, knowledge, discrimination are you"r gifts to us. You are not far. You are not near. *You are within us all.*

You are *our* Father and all of us are *your* children and no one is our adversary, nor is any stranger to us. Everyone is our friend. You are the benefactor of all living beings. You give us food, clothing, shelter, consciousness, wisdom, intelligence, beauty, wealth and honour." These are the fundamental teachings of Eastern, *i.e.,* Japanese or Indian Insights. Let us develop such a global consciousness of universal *brotherhood* and global citizenship in our organization. Indian Insight Stresses Spirit (Subtle), and Western Ethos focuses matter (gross). Let us have union of science and spirit or mind and matter.

Indian ethos has advocated *'Karma Yoga:* doing our work without hankering over fruits of our work. This healthy mind-set purifies our mind and heart and at the same time it gives benefit to our organization and our society. *This will also develop our global consciousness.*

****

13

Impact of Globalization on Cross-border Capital Flows: Emerging Trends

A. B. Lal

Globalization has become the order of the day. By globalization we mean 'integrating' the economy of a country with the world economy. It refers to the growing economic interdependence among countries, which is reflected in the increasing cross-border flow of goods, services, capital and know-how. Almost every country of the world is now adopting the policy of globalization. India adopted the policy of globalization in 1991 by opening up its economy to foreign portfolio and foreign direct investment (FDI) by providing facilities to foreign companies to invest in different sectors of the economy in a phased manner; removing constraints and obstacles to the entry of MNC's in India; allowing Indian companies to enter into foreign collaborations in India and also encouraging them to set-up joint ventures abroad as well as acquisitions and mergers of foreign business enterprises; carrying out massive import liberalization programmes by switching over from quantitative restrictions to tariffs in the first place and then bringing down the level of import duties consistently.

* Head, Department of Commerce, Meerut College and Dean, Faculty of Commerce and Business Administration, C.C.S. University, Meerut, India.

The concept of Globalization can be explained in several other ways depending on the level we choose to focus on. The underlying philosophy is, "the whole world is my market; wherever the opportunity arises I will tap it irrespective of location, standard of economy, ethnic relations and all other parameters." "Cross border customers are my neighbours; I will be close to them at any time". At the level of a specific country, globalization refers to the ability of the country to expand its trade and aggressively dominate in other parts of the world; by motivating its entrepreneurs.

Dr. R. Chandran in his famous book 'International Business', writes, "Despite the fact that globalization is taking place very rapidly, all the countries are not equally integrated into the global economy still. Some key indicators to measure the global integration of any country's economy are exports and imports as a ratio of GDP, inward and outward flow of foreign direct investment and portfolio investment, and flow of royalty and know-how payments associated with technology transfer. The growth of China and India with respect to some of these indicators during the last two decades ensures that they will emerge as major global players."

Since the end of the World War II, the rising tide of free-market ideology that started with developed economies has swept up South Korea, Taiwan, Hong Kong, Singapore and other South East Asian economies, and is now moving into China, India, Brazil, parts of Africa and Central and eastern Europe including Russia. The economic centre of gravity is shifting from the developed to developing countries. Economic liberalization and globalization promotes competition, efficiency, innovation, new capital investment and faster economic growth. Today's market mechanisms have allowed the developing economies to start catching up with the advanced economies, so that China, India, South Korea, Taiwan, Indonesia and Thailand are emerging as major players in the global market. In fact Taiwan, Hong Kong and Singapore, which were amongst the world's poorest countries in the 1950s, are already listed as advanced economies. Despite short-term disruptions, like the Asian financial crisis, the projections of long-term growth for the region are still valid. In the changing world scenario after World War II, there is a growing pervasiveness of the transnational corporations which see the entire world as a single market for production and marketing of goods and services.

The globalised or transnational economy is shaped mainly by money flows rather than by trade in goods and services. These money flows have their own dynamics. The monetary and fiscal policies of sovereign governments increasingly react to events in the international money and capital markets rather than actively shape them. The multinational trade negotiations under the auspices of GATT/WTO have been liberalizing trade and investment. The decision making power is shifting from national state to the regional blocks (i.e. regional blocks like EC, NAPTA, SAFTA, ASEAN, etc.) A growing proposition of the world out put is traded internationally and the faster growth of trade, than the GDP, is bringing about world economic integration. This economic integration is reinforced by the massive cross-border capital flows. Money and capital markets have been increasingly becoming transnational and universally obtainable.

It may be useful to restate that broadly, there are two types of foreign investment, namely, foreign direct investment (FDI) and portfolio investment.

FDI refers to investment in a foreign country where the investor retains control over the investment. It typically takes the form of starting a subsidiary, acquiring a stake in an existing firm or starting a joint venture in the foreign country. Direct investment and management of the firms concerned normally go together.

If the investor has only a sort of property interest in investing the capital in buying equities, bonds, or other securities abroad, it is referred to as portfolio investment. That is in case of portfolio investments, the investor uses his capital in order to get a return on it but has not much control over the use of the capital.

Since the economic liberalization of 1991, there has been a surge in the FDI and portfolio investments in India. Since 1992, Indian Companies, satisfying certain conditions, are allowed to access foreign capital markets by Euro issues. GD Rs (Global Depositary Receipts)/AD Rs (American Depositary Receipts) and FCC Bs (Foreign Currency Convertible Bonds) are instruments issued by Indian Companies in the foreign markets for mobilizing foreign capital by facilitating portfolio investment by foreigners, specifically by FIIs (Foreign Institutional Investors) like Mutual Funds in Indian securities.

Foreign capital inflows continued to fuel the economic growth machinery as India received a massive $32 billion as capital inflows in the year 2005. While, Indian companies preferred to mobilize resources from abroad, at the same time, foreign investors also parked their money in India. In fact, in the recent survey conducted by global consulting firm, A. T. Kearney, India emerged as the second-best destination after China, replacing United States. However, one must not forget that the debt-creating component of these capital inflows has been the key driver.

Foreign inflows made its presence felt in all sectors, especially in the stock markets. FIIs pumped in $8.3 billion in 2004-05; and the figures for 2005-06 have already crossed $10 billion. A very important source of capital inflows was the record $21 billion remittances from Indians abroad. Outward movement of funds also witnessed an increase because of search for new markets and overseas Merger and Acquisitions activities by Indian firms. Despite their increase, non-debt creating inflows such as FDI, portfolio investment and remittances which have a lot of development aspects still are low compared to the size of debt-creating capital inflows. (See Table–1) But it is true that the year 2005 has had companies like Intel, Microsoft, Vodafone and others investing substantial FDI into India. One can hope that year 2006 would see not only India reverberating with radical increases in capital inflows, but would also see Indian companies investing aboard. The government needs to necessarily give emphasis to the out flows from the economy as this indicates the true acceptance of India abroad. (New Year Special Issue: *Business and Economy*)

Table–1: Components of Capital Inflows

Capital Inflows (in $ million)	2004	2005
Non-debt creating inflows		
Foreign Direct Investment	3,420	3,037
Portfolio investment	11,356	8,907
Debt creating inflows		
External assistance	–2,742	1,922
External Commercial borrowings	– 1,526	5,947
N R I deposits	3,642	–1,067
Other banking Capital	2,589	5,069
Short-term credits	1,420	3,792
Others	2,383	4,568
Total	**20,542**	**32,175**

Source : R B I (mid-year reviews)

According to a recent report of UNCTAD's (United Nations Conference on Trade and Development) world Investment Report, FDI in India, on an average was 45.2 crores dollars during 1985-95, which moved up to 340 crores in 2001, 345 crores in 2002, 427 crores in 2003, 534 crores in 2004. During these periods, reverse F D I of India to foreign countries was on an average, $2.5 crore during 1985-95 which moved up to 139.7 crores in 2001, 1107 crores in 2002, 913 crore in 2003 and 2222 crores in 2004.

The UNCTAD report points out that total amount of FDI for the world was 64800 crores in 2004 which was 2 percent higher than the previous year. The F D I for developing countries was 233000 crores which was 40 percent higher than the previous year and amounts to 36 percent of total F D I for the world as a whole in 2004. Tables–2 & 3 show country-wise comparative figures of F D I for the year 2004 showing India is still below the radar.

Table–2 : Top 10 F D I Destinations (Figures in $ billion)

World F D	64.8
U. S. A.	95.9
U. K.	78.4
China	60.6
Luxemburg	57.0
Australia	42.6
Belgium	34.4
Hong Kong	34.0
France	24.3
Spain	18.4
Brazil	18.2
India	5.34

Table–3 : Top 10 Countries Investing in India (Figures in $ Million)

Mauritius *	820
U S	469
Netherlands	196
Germany	143
Japan	122
U. K.	84
Singapore	64
Switzerland	64
South Korea	14
Others	300

Source : Economic Survey – 2004-05

* Most countries route their FDI through Mauritius to take advantage of special tax treaty.

Asia remains the most favourite destination of FIIs.

The Indian bourses (stock exchange) are on a historic roll, creating record after record of 2005 each day. The sensex has crossed 9600 in the beginning. And incidentally, it is not one of those isolated Indian success stories. In fact, Asian stock markets of many hues like the Hangren and the Nikkei too are in fire. Similarly, Malaysian markets, which saw a spurt in portfolio investments from $ 1·09 billion in 2003 to $ 8·89 billion in 2004, continue their party. The trend remains the same for Thailand (–$ 73 million in 2003 to $ 1·3 billion in 2004) and Indonesia ($ 1·22 billion in 2004 to $ 1·27 billion in 2004). Undoubtedly, the situations warrants questioning that whether this hot money is going to be staying put within these economies or is it paving the way for yet another Asian Crises?

It could be a redundant question, as the Asian crisis of 1990s erupted primarily on account of volatile short-term debts. And, it was not the FIIs, but the domestic investors who fled the economies of Thailand and Korea. A recent report by the Ashok Lahiri Committee to study the affect of FIIs in the Indian economy has highlighted interesting insights. It has found that it is actually the domestic investors who pulled out their money at the drop of the hat and the FIIs have actually been net buyers at the time of crisis. For instance, from 2000 to 2003, when Indian market was recovering from the IT slump, mutual funds were net sellers in the equity markets.

'So, looking at the trends of portfolio investment across the region, there is not any doubt that as long as the returns are healthy and the fundamentals of the economy, along with the technicals of the stock look-strong, the fore kitties of the Asian countries would bulge. Fair weather or rough weather, they are here to stay. Gone are the days when Uncle Sam would sneeze and the whole of Asia caught a cold' (*Business & Economy*, 30 Dec. 2005 to 12 January 2006)

China's low rank, ninth among 10 markets rated in the sixth annual corporate governance survey conducted by CLSA Asia-pacific markets and the Asian Corporate Governance Association should be of particular concern to investors at the bourses. China may be pulling in the bulk of the world's foreign direct investment, yet it punches well below its potential with the institutional investors. It is exactly the opposite of what India is experiencing. That goes a long way toward explaining why on the day the latest corporate governance survey was released, the Shanghai Stock Exchange Composite Index was down 13 percent on the year, while India's Bombay Stock Exchange sensex-30 Index was up 31 percent. China has a host of other problems. Its financial system in fragile and it's an open question whether the Communist party can continue creating the hundreds of millions of jobs needed to maintain political stability. China has a long way to go, as evidenced by the report focus on companies that don't measure up.

The surge in the cross-border private investment as a result of the global economic liberalization has resulted in a substantial change in the composition of the international capital flows and increase in the magnitude of FDI has remarkably changed the balance of payments and foreign reserves position of several countries specifically the Asian giants among developing countries China and India (see Tables–4, 5 & 6).

Table–4 : GDP (PPP): League of Industrial Nations in 2004 (Figure in $ billion)

U. S. (1)	11,750
China (2)	7,262
Japan (3)	3,745
India (4)	3,319
Germany (5)	2,362
U. K. (6)	1,782
France (7)	1,737
Italy (8)	1,609
Brazil (9)	1,492
Russia (10) G D P (Purchasing Power Parity) :	1,408
World	55,500
EU	11,650

Source : *C I A (The World Fact Book)*

Table–5 : Top 10 Largest Holders of Foreign Exchange Reserves (Figures in $ billion)

Japan	843 ·2 (as on Nov. 2005)
China	769 (as on Sep. 2005)
Taiwan	253 · 5 (as on July 2005)
Korea	205 ·6 (as on July 2005)
Russia	164 · 97 (as on Oct. 2005)
India	143 · 9 (as on Dec. 2005)
Hong Kong	121 ·8 (as on Oct. 2005)
Singapore	115 ·56 (as on Oct. 2005)
Germany	99 ·19 (as on Oct. 2005)
U. S	64 ·48 (as on Dec. 2005)

Table–6 : Global Trade (2004 estimates)

(Countries ranking in brackets)	**(Figures in $ billion)**	
Country	**Exports**	**Imports**
U. S. (1)	795	1476
U. K. (6)	347 ·2	439 4
China (3)	583 ·1	552 4
Russia (17)	162 ·	5 92 9
Brazil (28)	95	61
India (26)	69 ·2	89 3
Singapore (16)	174	155 ·2-
Malaysia (19)	123 5	99 3
Thailand (23)	87 9	80 8
Indonesia (34)	69 9	45
Philippines (39)	38 63	37 5

(Countries ranking in brackets)	**(Figures in $ billion)**	
Country	**Exports**	**Imports**
Vietnam (51)	23·7	26·3
Combodia (106)	2·3	3·1
Myanmar (118)	2·1	1·7
Laos (171) ·	36	57

Source: ***C I A the World Fact Book***

In an article in *Economic Times*, Swami Nathan Aiyar described how developing Asia in investing its large and growing forex surpluses in U. S. Treasury securities, depressing U. S. interest rates and forcing more of American Capital to venture into emerging markets to raise the rate of return. Since the form that such American Capital takes in equity investment, the result is to hike the level of foreign ownership of emerging market Companies. This is true of India as well. According to one report, overseas investors own a third of the equity capital of 50 Companies comprising the National Stock Exchange index, S&PCNX Nifty.

The agency supplying India's forex reserves to governments abroad via investment in their bonds is the Reserve Bank. Its mandate is not to maximize returns, but to minimize risk. The agencies recycling capital out of the industrial countries back to emerging markets are private investors: direct and portfolio. Private equity, pension funds, mutual funds and other collective investment schemes scour developing markets for investment opportunities. Their mandate is to take risks and maximize returns. So they buy into equity. An excessive forex hoard results from an economy's inability to absorb the savings available to it for investment.

India's forex reserves are built not so much by current account surpluses (in fact a modest current account deficit in

2004-05 is recorded) as by capital account inflows that are not absorbed by the real economy as imports of goods and ren.ises. When foreign investors bring in money to invest in stock or build steel plants, their dollars end up with RBI which gives them rupees instead. The same thing happens with borrowings abroad. This dollar hoard of RBI run down when Indians repay loans abroad, make investments abroad and import mere goods and service then they sell abroad. The way to reduce such recycling is to increase the claims on RBI's forex hoard, our entrepreneurs should acquire profit promising Companies abroad; let the Indian public invest in developed country equity more liberally and set-up investments in the Indian economy e.g. in infrastructure improvement so that more goods and services are imported and new enterprises may be set-up. The globalization has both positive and negative aspects. The country with efficient economic management will face less of negative aspects and more of the positive aspects.

****

14
Globalization and Social Change

Sanjeev Mahajan*

Change is law of nature as everything changes over a period of time. When the concept of change is extended to social sphere, it is called 'social change'. Social change is a word used to describe variations in or modifications of any aspect of social processes, social patterns, social interactions or social organization. In its most concrete sense social change means that large number of persons are engaging in activities that differ from those which they (or their immediate forefathers) engaged in sometime before. Society is composed of a vast and complex network of patterned human relationships in which all men participate. When human behaviour is in the process of modification, this is only another way of indicating that social change is occurring.

It is rightly said that all societies experience change—change in the way people make a living, in the way they relate to one another; in the values they hold. For example, pre-historic hunters and gatherers become farmers, and farmers become merchants and city dwellers; steam and electricity replace manpower, and industrial revolutions transform human life. Similarly, empires rise and fall. Democracies replace

* Department of Post-graduate Studies and Research in Sociology, N. A. S. College (CCS University), Meerut, India.

dictatorships; and dictatorships, democracies. The deepest values of one generation are rejected—even ridiculed—by the next generation. Through all these changes in human societies, a few things remain constant : the need to make a living, whether it is by subsistence farming or by directing a sophisticated atomic research program; the need for some form of social organization; the need for norms and values that direct behaviour; and the need for cultural expression in art, philosophy, and religion. Although these basic needs do not change, the ways in which they are met change continuity.[1]

1. Early Explanations of Social Change

It is but natural that social scientists have been closely interested in explaining the process of social change. In fact, this interest accelerated in 18th and 19th centuries due to rapid and violent changes in European societies. According to Bottomore[2], the Scottish historians and philosophers (in particular, Ferguson, Millar, and Robertson), the French philosophers (Voltaire, Turgot, Condorcet), the German historians and philosophers (Herder, Hegel), were all concerned to explain or interpret the social and political revolutions of their age, within the framework of a general theory of history. Their influence was profound and can be plainly seen in later writers such as Saint-Simon and Buckle, and in work of the first sociologists. Comte, Marx and Spencer. Even later in the 19th century, a historical and evolutionary approach was dominant in sociology and anthropology. All the early scholars were interested in explaining the phenomena of rise of modern Western capitalism, increasing rationalization of social life and its implications for human freedom.

In early explanations of social change, the notion of 'change', 'social evolution', 'social development' and 'social progress' are sometimes confused, are combined in a single concept of 'social change'. Even if attempt was made to distinguish these terms, they were treated as logically related terms. The notion of *'social evolution'* was an application of theories of biological evolution which, in the nineteenth century powerfully reinforced the influence of philosophy of history upon sociology. Charles Darwin's (1809-1882) pioneering work in biological evolution made an in-depth influence on social scientists. According to Darwin's approach, there has been a continuing progression of successive life forms. For example, since human beings came at a later stage of evolution than reptiles, we represent a 'higher' form of life.

Social theorists sought an analogy to this biological model and originated *evolutionary theory*, which views society as moving in a definite direction. Early evolutionary theorists generally agreed that society was inevitably progressing to a higher state. As might be expected, they concluded in an ethnocentric fashion that their own behaviour and culture were more advanced than those of earlier civilizations.[3]

Comte (1798-1857), the father of Sociology, was an evolutionary theorist of change. He saw human societies as moving forward in their thinking from mythology to the scientific method. Spencer (1820-1903) was first to propound an analogy between society and an organism in his book Social Statics (1850) and between social an organic growth. Tylor used this term in a very impressive way in his book Primitive Culture (1871) to trace the stage of development or evolution. Durkheim (1858-1917) maintained that society progressed from simple to more complex forms of social organization. The writings of these scholars are examples of unilinear evolutionary theory. This approach contends that all societies pass through the same successive stages of evolution and inevitably reach the same end. Modern writers like Ogburn[4] and Childe[5] have observed that the notion of social evolution as applied to social institution has produced few results which may be termed as significant. Still this term is in use in social sciences, particularly in Sociology to explain social change.

The term *'social development'* is as vogue as the notion of 'social evolution' in explaining social change. *Oxford English Dictionary* defines development as 'a gradual unfolding; a fuller working out of the details of anything; the growth of what is in the germ.' It is in this sense that we can speak of the development of a child, or of a disease. But it is difficult to speak in the same way of social development, for we cannot always, with any certainty, refer a particular phenomenon to its germ, or clearly distinguish in a particular process between development and decay. There are only two (related) social processes to which it seems possible to apply the term 'development' with any accuracy; namely the growth of knowledge and the growth of human control over the natural environment as shown by technological and economic efficiency. It is, indeed, these two processes which have figured most prominently in developmental or evolutionary accounts of human society.

The metaphor of 'growth' was employed in the notion of 'development' as put forward by early social scientists. Development was conceived of as organic, immanent, directional, cumulative and irreversible. Also it entailed the idea of structural differentiation and increasing complexity. Sharma[6] has rightly stated that with the rise of the industrial system and the emergence of capitalism there cropped up new Western development thinking. The central element of this new thinking was the idea of economic growth, measured in terms of growth of GNP. This shift in the meaning of development gained further impetus in the middle of the last century when so many countries of the third world attained freedom from colonial rule and confronted the problem of economic reconstruction. Thus the term development acquired a strong economic connotation, so strong as to become synonymous with economic growth. The works authored by Rostov and Hoselitz among others bear ample testimony to this shift in the meaning of development.

The connotations of social development in terms of 'economic growth', 'redistribution with growth' and 'improvement chances' also led many sociologists to make a distinction between two types of present day societies, on the one hand, industrial societies, and on the other hand, all the societies (of very different types in other respects) which are predominantly rural and agricultural, and have relatively low levels of income. It also referred to the process in which the latter are now being industrialized.

The fallacy with the meaning of social development in terms of economic development lies in the fact that it ignores its socio-cultural contexts. Industrialization, as it occurred in developed societies has an entirely different historical context than it is being pursued in the developing societies. Moreover, in pre-supposes that industrialization would provide solution to every problem in these societies. In fact, industrialization has failed to solve the basic problem concerning human welfare even in developed societies. It is true that these societies have become affluent, the living standards of their people have risen, literacy rate has increased, and expectancy of life has explosion in the field of scientific knowledge and technology.

The conceptions of 'social evolution' and 'social development' are intimately connected with the idea of *'progress'*. Progress implies the growth in a particular sphere of social life. Comte, Spencer and Hobhouse have used the term progress. However, this concept coincides with development in early writings. Since the end of the 19th century the idea of progress has fallen into disfavour or neglect, not only in sociology but more generally in the Weltanschauung of intellectuals in Western societies.

In this respect, there is an immense difference between the Western industrial countries and the low income countries in most of the rest of the world. In the latter the evils of poverty, ill-health, ignorance, and sometimes oppression are still almost untouched, and as C. P. Snow has recently observed it is absurd for Western intellectuals to expound their own skepticism concerning progress to the people or political leaders of such countries. There, at least, the line of progress is unmistakable, and sociologists in particular would be well occupied in studying the various pre-conditions for over-coming the present great (and increasing) disparity in levels of living between rich and poor countries.[7] While accepting the notion of progress in terms of man having increased ability to master the environment, it may be argued that this trend has increased human happiness or has produced societies that are better at filling their members' emotional and psychological needs. Our ability to travel faster than the speed of sound does not mean that we have mastered the art of living.

2. Westernization and Modernization as Explanations of Social Change

Social change has also been explained by such terms as 'Westernization' and 'modernization'. These two terms, oftenly considered synonym as Western countries are also modern, have explained social change in different spheres of social life better than the earlier conceptions of evolution, development and progress. Westernization refers to a process of change which a non-Western country undergoes as a result of prolonged contact with a Western one. M. N. Srinivas[8] used this term 'Westernization' to characterize the changes brought about in Indian society and culture as a result of over 150 years of British rule, and the term subsumes changes occurring at different levels—technology, institutions, ideology, values. Similar, changes were brought about in other developing countries as a contact with Western culture. However, this has been a narrow concept as it applied only to the changes in developing societies. On the contrary, modernization has been a wider concept.

When we say that a society is 'modern', we are referring especially to the related phenomena of industrialization and urbanization and the great changes they have brought to community life. The second of the great natural revolutions of man, the industrial revolution (the first was the urban revolution), began in England in the late 18th and early 19th centuries. Industrialization has had a striking effect on the growth of cities; it started what might be called a second urban revolution which has led to the huge metropolitan areas and urban-dominated societies of the present day. Only the nations of Western Europe and the United States began to modernize as early as the 19th century. Most nations have started only recently, and many still remain rural and agricultural societies today.

Contemporary social scientists use the term modernization to describe the far-reaching process by which peripheral nations move from having traditional or less developed institutions to those characteristics of more developed societies. Many sociologists are quick to note that terms such as modernization and even development contain an ethnocentric bias. The unstated assumptions behind these terms are that 'they' (people living in developing countries) are struggling to become more like 'us' (in the core industrialized nations). Viewed from a conflict perspective such use of modernization and development perpetuates the dominant ideology of capitalist societies.

Contemporary sociologists emphasize that both industrialized and developing countries are 'modern'. (Indeed, developing countries are inextricably lined to the economies of core nations through colonialism, neo-colonialism, and the activities of multinational corporations). Current researchers are increasingly viewing modernization as movement along a series of social indicators—among them, degree of urbanization, energy use, literacy, political democracy, and use of birth control. Clearly, these are often subjective indicators; even in industrialized nations, not all observers would agree that wider use of birth control represents an example of 'progress'.

Keeping in view the post-modern era of American and Western societies, even the concept of 'modernization' has become less important in explaining social change around the world. The unprecedented phenomenon of an alteration of the relationship of basic economic relations between nations with reference to trade, investment, intellectual property rights and other basic areas of transnational economic activity occurred in the last few decades changing the world scenario, required another concept for explaining change as a result of these activities. Here the concept of 'globalization' comes into existence to explain wide ranging changes throughout the world.

3. Globalization as an Explanation of Change

The term 'globalization' is a multidimensional concept that refers to the transformation of trade, technology, industry and economy in a universalizing direction. Globalization views the entire world as a single market; it does not differentiate between domestic market and foreign markets. In other words, there is nothing like a home market and international market—there is only one market, i.e. the global market. It refers to the policy of opening country's doors for foreign investors, reducing import duties and protecting the interests of foreign investors. It is a free flow of goods, ideas and people across the globe. Globalization defined as a combination of internationalization, political and economic liberalization and a technical revolution, offers to policy-makers new opportunities but also powerful reason to worry about how they might manage both globalization and its impact.

The world is being globalized every day. As the world shrinks people are developing more similarities to one another and the world is caught in a paradigm of socialization between different cultures and societies. When one travel's the world, they can usually find a McDonald's, an Irish pub, and/or a

Chinese restaurant. Customs, norms, beliefs, and traditions are being exchanges as travel becomes more accessible and information is easier to access.

While the history of globalization can be debated, it must be nonetheless admitted that the rapidity with which the globalization pounds against the states has become increasingly server at the beginning of 21st century. Globalization is a worldwide trend and it is unstoppable. It is caused by three prime movers—economic globalization, technological globalization and political globalization. The three prime movers initiated a process in which geographic distance becomes less a factor in the establishment and sustenance of border crossing, long distance, economic, political and socio-cultural relations and which we call globalization. However, globalization has different meanings to different people. Some thinkers view it as the process of advancement of human beings, while some view it as the process of social integration and human insecurity. Globalization has been viewed as neo-imperialism, homogenization, hybridization and as cosmopolitanism.

Globalization is not an especially new phenomenon when discussed in terms of integration of territorial economies. Nevertheless, the current phase has a certain remarkable characteristics that are 'the annihilation of space through time'. This phase seems to have some novel consequences in the social/cultural sphere; some argue convergence of social spaces and others argue more divergence.

One aspect of today's globalization is the accelerated development of information-communication-technology (ICT), followed by growing polarization between those who do and those who don't have access to ICT. ICT holds a promise for enhancing social equity, by making information and knowledge. The important resources of 21st century global society-accessible to all. If, however, some groups in society are excluded from this, this promise turns into a threat and inequalities are but growing. This is 'the digital divide' phenomenon, which has been gaining growing attention and research.

Singh[9] has delineated five dimensions of globalization – (1) revolution in communication technology rendering global circulation of messages and symbols in the shortest time possible and proliferation and diversification of technological means for doing so; (2) circulation of financial capital on global scale searching for makers and economies of scale through international division of labour and structure of wages introduction of high technology; (3) homogenization of consumer products and market processes both in the realms of commodities and cultural symbols, styles and behavioural patterns; (4) enlargement of the scope of electronic media through telephony, television, fax, e-mail, Internet, etc., putting enormous new pressures on traditional notions of sovereignty and autonomy of states or governments impacting deeply on political values, ideologies and movements; (5) very high and intense degree of circulation of manpower across countries and cultures creating articulate and culturally sensitive diaspora of migrant population contributing to homogenization of cultures on the one hand, and to elevated sense of cultural identity and distinctiveness on the other.

4. Globalization and Social Change

Globalization has tremendous capacity to generate change in different spheres and change the life styles of the people throughout the world. It does usher many technological, economic, ecological and social changes in society which affect the traditional cultural styles, forms and ideologies. At one side globalization has created a number of opportunities to those who are competent, ambitious and real businessmen. Globalization expands the opportunities for unprecedented human advances, sustainable development and poverty reduction. India and other countries can derive the maximum benefits by globalizing their economies in the many areas at reasonable prices as we have rich human resources. On the other side, recent studies show that globalization has posed threats to employment livelihood of poor people, environments and human security. Globalization is synonymous to competition and strength. Naturally, in the process of globalization, the developing countries and the least developed countries, are still unprepared for accepting the challenge of global market and are lagging behind the developed countries.

Scholars like Singh[10], Kothari[11], Krishna Kumar[12], Peggy Mohan[13] among many others have discussed far-reaching cultural potential of globalization for Indian society, which still remains largely a nation of peasants and working classes totalling about 70 percent of population. For example, Singh[14] has stated that some of its effects upon the regional and national cultures may be modernizing but there are significant areas where it has a disruptive influence upon the local culture. For example, globalization of markets has led to conversion of traditional objects of art and aesthetics having mostly ritual uses in the local communities into marketable commodities. This has not only rapidly disrupted the autonomy of folk cultures, but also destabilized the life of the artisans by creating new networks of competition and price war and a new class of exploitative middle men. In other areas, such as access of local communities to forest resources, land and rivers, hills and lakes, all of which were bounded together in a long enduring cultural ecology of rituals and customs, the penetration of market for profit has started a rapid subversion of ecology. It has disrupted the balance in the cultural, social and economic life of many communities including tribes, artisans, traditional cultural performers, etc. Being in minority and economically vulnerable, these communities suffer loss of their cultural identity the most in the process of globalization.

Globalization of communication in terms of electronic media (radio, television, computer networks, internet, etc.) has empowering impact on the local communities and cultures, which are inspired by the new telecommunication media to reassert their cultural identity and reinforce their resilience. It helps them maintain their identity by accessing themselves to cultural meanings and values rather selectively through an adaptive mechanism. Thus, globalization enhances the consciousness of cultural identity.

The fear that globalization will suppress the voice of the down-trodden, multi-national companies will prevail over local industries and India will be pushed into the financial dependency seems to be unfounded. It is true that it may lead to job crunch, increase the disparities between haves and have-nots, increase the importance of private sector, and threaten the local folk culture and identity of the people in a developing country like India. However, the process of globalization is quite new in Indian society and its impact, both negative and positive, cannot be felt so soon.

Notes and References

1. Ronald C. Federico, *Sociology,* California : Addison-Wesley Publishing Company, 1975, p. 659.
2. T. B. Bottomore, *Sociology : A Guide to Problems and Literature,* London : Unwin University Books, 1969, p. 263.
3. Richard T. Schaefer and Robert P. Lamm, *Sociology,* New Delhi : Tata McGraw-Hill Publishing Company Limited, 1999, p. 600.
4. W. F. Ogburn, *Social Change,* New York : Huebsch, 1922, p. 57.
5. V. Gordon Childe, *Man Makes Himself,* London, 1956, pp. 16-17.
6. S. L. Sharma, "Changing Conceptions of Development" in Dharam Vir and B. P. Sharma (eds.), *Socio-Cultural*

Development : A Global Perspective, New Delhi : Classical Publishing Company, 1989, pp. 1-2.

7. T. B. Bottomore, Op. Cit., p. 268.
8. M. N. Srinivas, *Social Change in Modern India*, Berkley : University of California Press, 1966, p. 47.
9. Yogendra Singh, *Culture Change in India : Identity and Globalization*, Jaipur : Rawat Publications, 2000, pp. 71-72.
10. Yogendra Singh, Op. Cit.; and *Significance of Culture in the Understanding of Social Change in Contemporary India*, Presidential Address, New Delhi : Indian Sociological Society, 1994.
11. Rajni Kothari, "Globalization and Revival of Tradition : Dual Attack on Model of Democratic Nation-Building", *Economic and Political Weekly*, 1995, p. 50.
12. Krishna Kumar T., "Management of Development in the Newly Emerging Global Economic Environment", *Economic and Political Weekly*, 1996, p. 50.
13. Peggy, Mohan, "Market Forces and Language in Global India", *Economic and Political Weekly*, 1995, p. 50.
14. Yogendra Singh, Op. Cit., p. 50.

****